GET IT !

The Complete Guide to Becoming The Ultimate You...

By: Brett Figueroa

GETTING IT is the most important function to living…

There will be many opportunities to GET IT here…

Welcome…

Come on in.….

Photo By: Jen Henningsen/www.keepsakephotographypics.com

Cover Design: Carmel Legacy/carmel@elenajane.com

Editor: Mike Valentino/www.editor-ghostwriter.com

Dedication

This book is dedicated to those committed to doing whatever it takes to make their life a true masterpiece, a fantasy of possibilities and true commitments. It's dedicated to those who MUST GET IT right now; the ones who do not have time to sift through 800 pages of information to get it, they must get it in quick, tight, fast pieces. It's also dedicated to those willing to get off whatever is and has been holding them back from succeeding at the highest level, no matter how great you're doing. I also dedicate this book for the times - the times we're in today - not yesterday and not next week, today. In these times we are facing today it is easy to want to dodge and hide, yet the real power here will be to face things head-on with a deeper sense of power. Someone once told me, "Brett, you can only go for so long pretending you don't have a cavity, it'll catch up to you." In the commitment to face today's challenges I also dedicate this book to those who are willing to step up to the plate right now - not later - right now to turn things around, and to better your own life. This book is also dedicated to those daring few that no matter where they are absolutely believe they too can succeed beyond their wildest dreams. It's for the few who do versus the many who talk. This book is also dedicated to those not just sick and tired of being where they are, yet those *sick and tired of being sick and tired of where they are,* as being sick and tired is just not enough. This book is dedicated to those committed to creating the freedom that so few enjoy, the freedom to embrace the true self. This book is for those willing to take full responsibility to roll up their sleeves, dig in, and get after it. It's for the believer. It's for the contributor in you. This book is dedicated to those willing to face up to their ultimate fears and break-through to the other side, the side that holds the prize. This book is for the underdog, the unsung hero, the 2% of the world population that has the heart to win, the guts to go for it and the courage to take a shot! Lastly, this book is dedicated to the people of the world that have been knocked down, kicked down, pushed down, thrown down, pulled down and are willing to pull themselves up by the bootstraps and get busy, really busy.

Special thanks to my amazing wife and three children. Garrett, Grant and Gannon. You are my pride and joy, the love of my life. You each have postponed having a daddy while this book was being written and I am forever grateful; I owe you some trips. To my wonderful, amazing wife Shelley who also participated as co-editor and late night ear, you rescued me, and you are the love of my life. This book would not have been possible if it was not for the space you created in our home, I thank you and I love you.

I also dedicate this book to my early mentors and role models, such as Joe Tishkoff, Baron O'Brien, Jim and Gina Penn, Bob Newman, Tony and Sage Robbins, Marty and Ed Rodriguez, Jim and Tammy Meyer, Dan Lier, Curtis Kessinger, and all those who have supported my work.

A special acknowledgement to Oprah Winfrey for being the light of possibility for so many and an inspiration for this book, I thank you with all my heart. Thank you to Joel Osteen for sharing a piece of yourself each and every Sunday morning to lift my family's spirits and allow for us to be all that we can be; we thank you. I would also like to dedicate this book to my A Team players, who have given so much of their time and energy to living an outstanding life and making a contribution. This book would not be possible without you, and I am forever grateful.

I praise and give thanks to our amazing cover designer, Carmel Legacy, our fantastic do whatever it takes editor Mike Valentino, our photographer Jen Henningsen and our fast as lightning printers.

And most importantly, I give thanks to GOD for giving me life every day. Here is some homework, I hope you like it.

YOU ARE A RARE BREED...

Congratulations for picking up this book. If you're committed, it can transform your life; literally turn a life from bottom down to right side up. It can take someone from doing great to doing OUTSTANDING and it can take them there, immediately. I have seen it work all over the USA and abroad. These skills, reminders, philosophies and cutting edge strategies will catapult you into another stratosphere, literally a universe of your own and take you to far away places traditionally only the privileged have enjoyed, till NOW. Your time has come, time to be all that you can be and more. It's time to step into the places, reach into the crevices and pull out the best of what you've got, the best of who you are, everything you can be. It's time to become even more. Welcome.

Man's in his yard searching for his keys when his neighbor came over asking to assist. After several minutes passed without successfully finding the keys the neighbor finally asked "Are you sure you lost your keys out here?" "Well no, silly; I lost them inside." "INSIDE!!! Why are we out here then?" "Well, it's just too dark inside."

GREAT, Let's Turn on Some lights...COME ON IN...

You have dreams, you have visions, you have goals and you have fantasies, but it's just been too dark inside for you to find them. You have a fantasy that all your dreams come true, come about, come to realization. At night you lie awake thinking about the GOOD LIFE and how great that would be for you and your family, you have a deep fantasy that you are more than you are demonstrating, more than what meets the eye. You know you have all it takes. You know it's been there the whole time and you also know you can do it, you have been there before. You know you are strong, powerful and confident. You know you can lose those extra 20 pounds, you know you can turn your marriage around, you know you can upright your finances, you know you can regain emotional mastery, you know you can! You know you can reshape your life, reshape your beliefs, reshape your thoughts; you know you can move from procrastination into action and you know fear is false. You know you have the eye of the tiger deeply imbedded in your infinite spirit and you also know when to seize opportunity. You know this is that opportunity. Whatever your dreams, whatever those fantasies, no matter how far-out there they are, no matter how ridiculous or out of the boundaries, it's time to live them and it's time to become all that you were meant to be. Welcome to GET IT…

Your Question, Bob?

When I am conducting live events it's an open forum. Step up any time I say. Ask ANY question, no softballs please. The event is going as planned, everybody's cool, no questions; things carry on…till Bob on aisle 32 has a question. Bob stands up, grabs the nearest microphone and proceeds with his question. I take the question, process and search for an immediate solution. I am clear no matter what Bob comes to the table with we can handle it. I jump off the stage into the audience and get directly in front of Bob. Bob has something he's not clear on, he's looking for clarity so he can have his life work more effectively and I'm there to give it. We don't have time to pull out books, research papers, data, notes, etc., yet he needs the answer immediately and now. Bob will be stuck unless Bob gets to the answer. I've got 30 seconds to one minute to GET to the resolve, to hit the bull's eye, there's a live audience watching, there's lots at stake. In one bullet, one metaphor, one example, one quick tight story, Bob is handled; he's got what he was looking for. He was caught up in sorting data, information, theories and concepts, we broke it down so it makes IMMEDIATE SENSE, he's no longer stuck…he GETS IT instantly.

"Bob, you GOT it, right?"

"GOT it, Brett, thanks!"

"Great, have a seat".... audience applauds…

This book is written that way. The way in which you'll instantly GET what you must GET so you can carry on with YOUR event. There are "GOT ITs" at the end of each subchapter and questions to move you along quicker and easier. The book also does not necessarily read linear, it reads as you would like to read. Keep it on your nightstand; it makes for a great resource book. Lastly, the quotes throughout are designed to tell the story, sum it up and encapsulate the content. They're the hand-grenade, the BOMB and they GET to the point faster than writing a whole page. It hits you at the core, you'll GET IT faster. Pay extra special attention to these.

I know you've heard it ALL before….

We are intelligent people; we know what to do and not to do to succeed in our lives. We've studied, we've researched, we know. I know for the most part you've heard all this stuff before, I know that. You know in order to succeed you must first GET excited then GET committed and then do whatever it takes, make it happen, you know -- the same-old same-old. Blah, blah, blah, I'm preaching to the choir.

Here's the deal - listening and reading this stuff is like flying on an airplane. For those who have flown, when we board the aircraft we find our seat assignment, put our stuff in the compartments overhead and grab a seat, simple. We have some idle chit chat with our fellow passengers; look through our handbags and make any last minute calls…all while the flight attendant is giving life-saving tips in case of an emergency, she tells us where to go and what to do, with exact precision in case of that emergency. We don't listen; we hear nothing, it's a waste of time, we cannot be bothered, we have been down this path before. I have been flying since I was 10 I think to myself. What is she going to say that I don't already know, I mean really, I've heard this stuff so many times I could recite it by rote. I know exit door to the left, exit door to the right..yada yada yada……Can we just get on with it, can we just go….I've got some music to listen in on and some papers to read.

We sit there patiently. Time stops. Ah, the moment we have been waiting for, TAKE OFF! We depart the gate and begin to back up, we know we're on our way to hitting the runway, we adjust our seats in that uncomfortable upright position, we glance out the window and we overhear that we are next for takeoff, whew. Rolling down the runway at about 150 miles per hour we feel moved, exhilarated and safe at the same time. As we ascend into the night sky rising to 15,000 feet we readjust, lean back and get comfortable. Peering out the window without a concern in the world and out of the blue we hear a loud THUNDEROUS BOOM from the right side of the plane near the engine, a flash ignites, the plane tilts slightly. The passengers gasp…oh S#@t what just happened; the worst is feared, we immediately think of our families, we are terrified. The captain comes on, you can hear panic in his voice… "ladies and gentlemen please listen up, we have just lost a right engine, we are going in for an emergency landing…here's what you MUST do to survive this landing," he says loudly……

How would you pay attention?

How fast would you GET IT?

We would pay attention as if our life depended on it, we would miss nothing, we would catch it all, every word, every syllable, EVERYTHING. There's nothing we wouldn't GET.

Participate fully

Isn't it true that life kind of shows up this way? It's all going great till it's not going great. Sitting with our lives comfortably relaxed back, peering out the window of life and BAM!! The invitation here is to not wait till the captain comes on in life and says... "Ladies and gentlemen, we're coming in for a divorce," "We're coming in for a bankruptcy," "We're coming in for cancer."

Grab it NOW, you'll be glad you did. GET what you must GET in order to elevate your life, expand your experience and be safe in your landing.

Get It! ~ Brett Figueroa

CONTENTS

Quick Reminder

PART ONE

TAKE FULL RESPONSIBILITY

Most would rather be partially responsible and blame the rest on the postman, the economy and or their parents.

1) **YOUR ABILITY TO RESPOND**…*Get it? Respond-Ability*
2) **QUIT THE BLAMING GAME**…*He did it, she did it, they did it…*
3) **YOU HAVE THE MOST AT STAKE HERE**…*It's your life, not mine, it's your vacations, not mine, it's your dreams, not mine…*
4) **LET GO NOW**…*It's ok, you've had it long enough…*
5) **GET OFF YOUR STORY**…*Yeah yeah yeah…*
6) **CHANGE WHO YOU'RE BEING**…*For most this will do it right here…*

PART TWO

GET UP AND GET COMMITTED

Most have wanted way too long and committed way too less, time to get committed.

Success is simple, not easy

1) **WHAT ARE YOU COMMITTED TO?** *Time to sign on the dotted line...*

2) **WANTING IS NOT ENOUGH**...*I want this...this...this, oh and this.*

3) **DECIDE TODAY**...*Once one decides to succeed the HOW to succeed shows up, it's like magic.*

4) **AS SOON AS**...*It stops raining, as soon as the economy turns around, as soon as I finish reading this book...then I'll really GET after it...as soon as!*

5) **REFORMATTING OUR LIVES**...
"Did you say I can start fresh?" "WOW! Just like when it was new..."

6) **BACK TO THE DAILY BASICS**...*Up   and   at   'em, Sunshine...Let's move it!*

7) **YOU CAN SUCCEED**...*That's a given, it's not as if you can't.*

PART THREE

TURN YOUR SHOULDS INTO MUSTS

This is a must

1) **RAISING YOUR STANDARDS**…*Raises Your Life*

2) **IT WILL FIND YOU**…*The Universal Tracking System*

3) **FLEX YOUR EMOTIONAL MUSCLES**…*Get a grip on this*

4) **WANT MORE TIME?** *Here…I'll show you how!*

5) **PLAYING THE GAME**…*If you're not getting beat up, banged up and bruised up you're not playing the game, you're playing it safe…*

PART FOUR

GET EXCITED AGAIN!

I just was excited; you mean I've got to do it again, yep! This time stay there.

1) **90% OF SUCCESS IS GETTING AND STAYING EXCITED**…*Here…I'll show you what I mean…*

2) **DRIVING FROM YOUR PASSION**…*YOU know…YOUR passion!*

3) **TODAY LET'S FIND OUT WHY?** *Success is simple…80% is WHY and 20% is How, most spend 20% on Why and 80% on How…oops!*

4) **YOU CAN HAVE IT ALL**… *"You mean it's not just this or that?"*

5) **TAKE CONTROL BACK**… *"You mean I can have control?"*

PART FIVE

DO WHATEVER IT TAKES

Most do whatever is convenient and then talk about how easy it is…

1) **WHAT AM I NOT WILLING TO DO**….*Gosh, I'm glad you asked…I won't do this… this…this…this, oh and this!*

2) **ACT AS-IF…**

Yeah, but I don't know how…

3) **BE A TWO-PERCENTER…**

2% will do whatever it takes to succeed and 98% can't be bothered

4) **#1 PRIMARY BELIEF…** *"Oh I see, just do whatever it takes, WOW, it's that simple?"*

5) **#2 PRIMARY BELIEF…***There's Always a way…*

6) **GET IN YOUR BEST PHYSICAL SHAPE**…*It's going to take a lot, you must be ready…*

7) **JUST SHOW UP…**

"You mean just show up?"

Yeah!

PART SIX

BUILDING STRONG DAILY HABITS

Habits are too light to be felt until too heavy to be broken…GET AN AX!!

1) **INCANT YOURSELF TO SUCCESS**…*Do it over and over till YOU BELIEVE it!!!*

2) **INVENT YOUR LIFE THROUGH QUESTIONS**…
"You mean if I ask myself better questions I'll have a better life?" Yes…

3) **BREAK YOUR LIMITING PATTERNS**… *Quit doing the same thing, that's insane…*

4) **YOU DON'T HAVE TO DO THIS**… *"Wait a minute…I thought I HAD to do all this??" Of course not, silly…come see what I mean…*

5) **WHAT'S NEXT FOR YOU?** *So, where do you go from here? …*

Bonus Material:

THE MOTIVATED MIND OF A 7 YEAR OLD, GRANT FIGUEROA…*Building future generations to come.*

BRETT GETS INTERVIEWED… *"Brett, the microphone's on…."*

Quick Reminder…

If it was easy, anybody could do it…

We know intuitively that reaching success in our dreams is not going to be easy; it's going to be a reach and a daily stretch. We also know few will survive this process. We've just GOT to remind ourselves right out of the gate. We can't be delusional and think otherwise. Sure we'll share with you skills, tools and ideas to assist in making it a bit easier, just as there is a nail gun to a hammer, yet one still must GET out there and make it happen. If success was easy anybody could do it. That's why most marriages fail, most bodies fail and that's why most people's dreams are shattered. It's not easy and they just quit, out of nowhere they just throw in the towel; they thought it was going to be easy or easier and they thought opportunities would just unload and when it doesn't work out that way they just quit. That's right, they up and quit. They quit even before they quit if you know what I mean. They quit the marriage; quit the dreams, quit the gym, they just up and quit. We emotionally quit first, then physically. In your pursuit you're going to want to quit a million times over; it's ok, it's part of the challenge, it's not as if it's supposed to be easy. We know otherwise. The question is, can you pass the test, can you make it through the obstacle course or will you just quit like so many? It's ok to want to quit, just don't, keep after it, follow it through, and make it happen. Whatever it is, go for it. There will be obstacle courses, one after another in fact…they'll keep coming at you…most give up, and they fall to the side. Most up and coming bodybuilders want to quit a million times over, most marriages at some point want to quit every 15 seconds, most every business wants to quit right after start up and every dreamer wants to quit, cave in, give it up. There is no way around this. The universe chews and spits up people's dreams all day long, either you're committed to them or you're not.

One must be sick and tired of being sick and tired in order to change.

Most just don't have the staying power. They stay with it till it's no longer convenient to stay, then they're out of there. Realizing your dreams is not going to be easy, you're going to take some hits, some blows, and some setbacks. There's going to be some disappointments and finger pointing, it's going too be rough, and tough, you're going to think you can't go another inch, you're going to want to fold up those dreams and catch up with them down the road. … …you'll find out not everyone is going come to your rescue, not everyone will support you, not everyone will believe in you. People will say you're wasting your time and GET a life. You will have your critics and people who pass judgment. Every outside distraction will be there to derail you, to set you back into mediocrity. You will find your comfort zone growing faster than your stomach, it will be nauseating, and you'll wish you were dead.

Few survive this process, most quit and die broke. Broke in their marriage, broke in their finances, broke in their confidence, broke in their disciplines, broke in their dreams, just dead broke.

You are special, you keep on; you know it's worth it, you know the late nights and early mornings are all worth it, you live in the fantasy of being seconds, just feet away from your pot of gold, you know there is a celebration in store. You think to yourself PRESS ON and you know you are guided….

Be Part of the Few who do versus the many who talk – most talk, few do.

PART ONE

TAKE FULL RESPONSIBLITY

Most would rather be partially responsible and blame the rest on the postman, the economy and or their parents.

"What is GET it?" someone asked.

"It's a fast-paced, hand- grenade hitting, bullet dropping slap in the face invitation to take on life like never before, an invitation to STEP UP," said a recent reader.

"It's a bit of NLP, mixed in with lots of motivation without the hocus-pocus," said someone else.

"It's Tony Robbins' passionate, direct, hard hitting style," said yet another.

"It's packaged Zen," said even another.

"It's Brett's way of earning a living," suggested a fifth reader.

Success Simplified:

1) Do what others are unwilling to do
2) Handle what others are unwilling to handle

"It's 200 pages of madness to create saner weekdays," said someone else.

"It's a car," said another.

"A car?" The inquisitor was now totally bewildered.

"Just a car," the reader went on. "You can use it to GET where you're going faster or use it to explore new places."

"I see," said the inquisitor, still perplexed.

"Or," another reader said, "You can just lie down in front of it and let it run over you and then blame the car."

"GOT IT."

Do not make life a concept, theory or
understanding; make it a fun-filled,
action-packed experience.

YOUR ABILITY TO RESPOND

GET it? Respond-Ability

"THE ABILITY TO RESPOND!" shouted the trainer from the front of the training room. "GET IT? The ability to respond to any and all given situations!" - he continued to shout with a loud thunderous BOOM! The trainer was intense; his name was Dan and he didn't let up. All of my stories, alibis, and what I thought were bulletproof justifications on why my life was the way it was, were being poked, prodded and exposed. I wanted OUT, I could not take another minute of this! This event promised miracles and all I was GETting was, "TAKE RESPONSIBILTY FOR MY LIFE". *Give me a break* I thought. I came here to make money, increase my sales AND BE MORE POSITIVE. *This sucks, there's GOT to be an easier way to success.* He was exposing what I had spent so much time crafting and perfecting. The holes to my mere existence were being exposed; I did not like the trainer. I WOULD RESIST HIM, I WAS GUARDED. He wanted me to take responsibility for the place in which my boat had docked. *The storm GOT me here* I thought, it threw me to these rocks…I was ANGERED; I jumped to my feet and shouted from the back of the training room, "My family doesn't need me to take responsibility sir, my family needs me to make some money, NOW CAN WE GET ON WITH IT???" "YOU'LL MAKE MONEY WHEN YOU TAKE RESPONSIBILITY FOR HAVING NO MONEY!" Dan shouted. "I have no money because of the economy and times are tough." "DO YOU TAKE RESPONSIBILITY FOR HAVING NO MONEY? YES OR NO?" "Yes, but the industry I've been in for years has absolutely collapsed, it's tough out there you know." "NO YES-BUTS!" he shouted. "DO YOU TAKE RESPONSIBILITY FOR BEING IN THAT INDUSTRY? YES OR NO?" "Sir, I'm only in that industry because I didn't go to college and that's all that was available." "DO YOU TAKE RESPONSIBILITY FOR NOT GOING TO

Hunger:

Placing yourself into a position where you *must* succeed, not *should* succeed!

COLLEGE? YES OR NO?" "Yes, but I didn't go to college because I wasn't taught to go to college." "DO YOU TAKE RESPONSIBILITY FOR NOT LEARNING TO GO TO COLLEGE?"..*DAMN-IT.* This was hurting. It was useless, there was no point, I was GETting nowhere. I was not used to this, he was breaking me down, and he wanted me to be responsible to the core. He said my life would finally work the way I dreamed of when and ONLY when I took FULL RESPONSIBILITY for having my life work, period. I wanted shared responsibility. It was easier to be partially responsible and partially run over.

Dan the trainer asked me if I was responsible for being born. "No!" I yelled, "that's silly, that was my parents' deal, it was a weekend thing you know?" "Fine" Dan said. "You're right, it WAS your parents' thing…" I figured he was going to lay off now and just as I was about to assume my seat Dan inquired with even more of a shout to insure I GOT it. "ONE MORE THING," he said. "ARE YOU RESPONSIBLE FOR WINNING THE COMPETITION IN COMPETING FOR THE GRAND ENTRANCE TO LIFE?" "Yes," I said, "that was not an accident, that was ALL ME, sir." "YEAH, AND EVER SINCE THEN IT'S BEEN EVERYBODY ELSE'S FAULT, RIGHT?" Dan shouted. "WHEN ARE YOU GOING TO TAKE RESPONSIBILITY HERE?" I was dazed and confused, lightning was ignited, I was seeing it for the first time. It reminded me of riding a bicycle in how you don't GET it, till you GET it, when it all seems to click together and one finally GETs it. That was happening here. I had been deflecting. I had spent much of my whole life as victim, run over, I GOT it…I AM RESPONSIBLE FOR WINNING THE RACE, FOR BEING BORN AND ALL IN IT, it's my life. I could either be responsible or be run over, it was my choice. I would soon GET that there was no power in thinking anything less. I would gain FULL access to my own personal power by taking full responsibility for my life. I was guaranteed that from the trainer. Taking responsibility for where I was, where I am, and for where I'm going.

What are you sacrificing?

I know someone who sacrificed...

Are You?

I felt I was ready to take full responsibility. "ARE YOU RESPONSIBLE FOR HAVING YOUR LIFE WORK?" Dan said. "YES I AM!" I yelled from the back of the room…. I GOT teary eyed standing in front of the audience taking responsibility for my life, TAKING RESPONSIBILITY FOR HAVING IT WORK, TAKING RESPONSIBILTY FOR MY MERE EXISTENCE. It was liberating. I felt free. The audience exploded in cheers. I sat down and reflected.

GOT IT

When I am responsible, my life works; and when I am not responsible, my life does not work, it's simple. It's not that taking responsibility is a good thing or not a good thing; it's just about having our lives work. You can either be responsible or be run over, it's your life.

Quick Question

What could you take immediate responsibility for and have your life work the way you say you'd like to have it work? Could you take responsibility for having your marriage work top-notch? Could you take responsibility for becoming wealthy? Could you take responsibility for GETting in your best shape EVER? What could you take total responsibility for in having happen in your life?

QUIT THE BLAMING GAME…

He did it, she did it, they did it…

As I took my seat my mind raced like a 400hp engine thinking about how I had been blaming society, blaming the economy, blaming the parents, blaming the mood, blaming the luck, blaming the conditions,

Are you an example or a warning?

blaming the boss, blaming the policies, blaming the procedures, blaming the prices, blaming the times, blaming the education, blaming the circumstances, blaming the market, blaming the Republicans, blaming the Democrats, blaming everything other than my own commitment to do something about it, hence, the car ran over me. I had been blaming the train crossing through town, blaming the traffic, blaming circumstances. I was only noticing the one finger I had pointed out at everyone else, yet missing the other three fingers pointed in at me. I had always felt in life I'd been run over, time after time after time I had been done unto, I had been traced down, tracked down and simply run over. The dang train, the dang light, the dang economy, the dang prices, the dang cancellation, I was clear the universe was out to GET me, it had an ax to grind, it wanted to take me out. I would say it wasn't me it was society, it's not me it's the economy, it's not me it's that prices are too high, it's not me, they did it, it's not me it's that the job market is tough and it's brutal out there and times are hard, *haven't you heard*? I wasn't being responsible. I lived my life as the world owes me, pointing outward for it to pay up huge sums, huge dividends. Can't I GET some respect; after all, don't you know who I am? I wanted the world to serve me.

I sat there in quiet despair as I thought about how I had been blaming, pointing and deflecting. That's not being RESPONSIBLE. That's blaming, pointing and deflecting, and there is a difference.

I wanted what should be, not what was. I thought taxes should be lower, I thought my parents should have been nicer, I thought minimum wage was too low, I thought my house should have appreciated more, I thought those city lights should be better timed, I thought the train should come through town only on my day off, I thought gas prices should be lower. Oh, how I thought things should be different. I wanted what should be not what was. It should be sunny (yeah but it's not), it should be raining (yeah but it's not), taxes should be lower (yeah but they're not), my wife should cook more (yeah but she doesn't), my kids should appreciate me more (yeah, but they don't).

A leader is one who is willing to GET in the trenches with the followers, as to be the example.

GET a shovel...

What is *is* and what isn't *isn't* I began to learn. The point was to take responsibility for the "is" in our lives. When we can learn to deal with the "is" of life we're on our way. .....it <u>is</u> raining outside, deal with it; it <u>is</u> snowing outside, deal with it. Like the dealing in a card game, we can win or lose based on how we deal. *What <u>is</u> is what matters, what should be is what doesn't.*

GOT IT

Taking responsibility is about not blaming. Blaming others for where we are and the circumstances that prevail. Blaming is not good or bad, it just doesn't work for those committed to having their lives work.

Quick Question

Who are you blaming in your life? Is it the economy? Is it your spouse? Is it the boss? Is it the times? Is it education or credentials? Is it your past, your upbringing? Who else are you blaming? Look around, who is it? Fess up.

YOU HAVE THE MOST AT STAKE HERE...

It's your life, not mine. It's your vacations, not mine. It's your dream, not mine.

Years ago while climbing the ranks to success I would struggle with my hardhead and ego. I got it slowly, not quickly. I would mainly resist, drag my feet and firmly believe I had a better way. I would fold my arms and defend my righteousness, all with a smile and all while I struggled. One day I asked my coach which one of his clientele he stayed awake for at night, the one that kept his thoughts racing. He said "Brett, I don't stay awake for any of them, I sleep really really well." I was shocked, I was hoping I was the one he stayed awake for - figuring out how to fix my

"GETting it" is important, you must GET it! GOT it?

mess. *Where's the love* I thought. He used the example that if he was a doctor and had 500 high blood-pressure patients and he told them all the same thing about not eating salt, eat low fat foods, drink lots of water, etc… then he's done his job. "I would sleep well," he said, "their spouses may not, yet I would sleep great…" I thought that sounded hard and callused, yet what he was saying was it's their life and as much as he would love his patients, if they choose to eat salt that's their issue not his. He does not make their issues his issue. He did his job, he told them not to eat the salt and that it would kill them. What's he going to do - put a scoped rifleman on the neighbor's house to see if the patient is eating salt? I mean really, he said it would KILL! GET that -- they have the most at stake, it's their life. We must set little reminder clocks to make sure we don't forget to do the things necessary in order to have our lives work most effectively.

The same with us, we have the most at stake here.

I remind people it's their vacations in jeopardy, it's their health in jeopardy, it's their marriage in jeopardy, it's their lives. So one can GET that being responsible, not blaming, and being at stake is about them; or not GET it and carry on with their lives. They can GET it or not GET it. GETting it is important and even MORE important to those willing to be at the highest stake.

With so much at stake, put yourself at risk. Find a place in your life where you are committed to finally GETting it done - GETting done whatever you have been putting off, GETting to the other side, the side that holds the prize. What is that place for you? What would it mean to GET to that place? Maybe it's making a certain amount of money, or losing some weight or completing a project. You have the most at stake in GETting it done and not GETting it done. One of my friends reminded me that there was possibly millions at stake in getting this book done. He said you're leaving a lot on the table, not including the millions of lives we will transform. I did not want to listen to him tell me to write pages,

Imagine...

What could you do in 60 days with full and committed participation toward your life?

yet I knew there was just too much at stake in not following through. What do you have at stake?

In your own life what is costing you? Possibly millions right now because of not taking the necessary actions, doing the proper follow-through? What are you not doing that if you were doing your whole world would turn right side up, your life would magnify to the place you *dream* of. What are you leaving on the table and what kind of a lifestyle shift could you experience by taking that shot?

Publicly confess to be most at stake...

At stake means being at risk. Years ago a friend of mine said she was going to quit smoking, I said, "Great, who else have you told?" She said "no one." "No one," I said, "what's it a secret?" She said, "No, but just in case I don't follow through on the goal, then it will be ok because I did not tell anyone." I told her to be at stake and go tell 10 people you really admire and trust and tell them you are committed to quitting smoking. She did and 15 years later she has never again had a single cigarette. Years later when asked about quitting she said there were a couple people out of that group of 10 that she would never let down in a thousand years, she had too much at stake, her REPUTATION. What do you have at stake that would insure your success, guarantee your follow through?

Here's an invitation, when you finish reading this chapter immediately go tell 10 people or 10 million people what you're going to do, what you're committed to having happen, with no down-the-road excuses. Put yourself at stake; put your reputation on the line. I have found public confession usually works better than private confession. GET to the part of your life that you're committed to. As a coach and trainer we love the people we work with, yet again it's their life and if they choose to not GET IT, it's sad, but really, who has the most at stake?

It's not what happens to you, it's
what you do about it!

GOT IT

Being at stake is being at risk, the higher the risk the higher the
rewards.

Quick Question

What do you have at stake, both personally and professionally? How
much money are you leaving on the table, how much happiness are you
leaving behind, how much passion and excitement is being forgotten?
Write it out, GET your journal out and take notes on what you have at
stake and what it would mean to truly follow through and *live* your
dreams. There's too much at stake, go for the dream.

LET GO NOW...

It's ok, you've had it long enough...

Two Monks named Tanzan and Ekido were once traveling together
down a muddy road. A heavy rain was falling. As they came 'round a
bend, they met a lovely girl in a silk kimono and sash, unable to cross the
intersection because of the mud.

"Come on, girl," said Tanzan at once. Lifting her in his arms, he
carried her over the mud.

Ekido did not speak again until late that night when they reached a
lodging temple. Then he could no longer restrain himself. "We monks,"

#1 Costly Mistake:

Spending too much time studying the root, when one should be spending more time picking the fruit.

he said, "don't go near females, especially not young and lovely ones. It is dangerous. Why did you do that?"

"'I left the girl there," Tanzan replied. "Are you still carrying her?"

What are you still carrying around from your past that burdens you, weighs you down, takes your power away and keeps you away from living your dreams and goals? Ekido was weighed down with the way he thought things should have been, and Tanzan was freed on site. What could you free yourself from right this very minute because you decided to, because you decided to let go and regain your power? I have several friends that have spent years and years on therapist couches attempting to let go of issues, attempting to free themselves from the shackles of the well-worn past. I believe things can be let go in a moment, the moment we decide to let go.

Here's an exercise. Grab a pen or pencil and hold it above your head. Now really hold the instrument above your head with a light grip, now grip even tighter. Imagine the pen as all the stuff you are holding onto, feel its weight in your hand. Feel how heavy it is, all your stuff you're carrying around, do you FEEL it? Great… Now at the count of three let go and let the pen hit the floor, are you ready? Great…..one…two…..hold tight to the pen, hold even tighter, even tighter….THREE, let go. It should be on the floor, detached from you. Are you still holding it? If so, let it go. See how simple letting go is? Now go enjoy some lemonade. Letting go is really as easy as one…two…three. Remember you are the one holding it and you are the one that can count to three. You do not have to count to three years or 30 years. Just to three. You can hold on for three years and see how that works for you and your family. You can let go of your past failures, past mistakes, past regrets or you can cling, hold, and grasp - it's your choice, you're a big kid.

What if you were wrong?

In these times we must let go of old ways and embrace new ways, the times call for it and demand it.

Go through your emotional orange orchard and pick out all the experiences of your past that you would like to discard and hit the delete button, just like on your computer. Create a new miracle in your life by letting go of things that do not support you. Invent a new you and do it in a moment.

GOT IT

Letting go is as easy as one two three…or you can keep counting till you're dead and carry it with you to the grave.

Quick Question

What could you let go of that could free you, lighten your load or simply make life better? Are you willing to let that go? Great, then let it go…one two three….

GET OFF YOUR STORY…

Yeah, Yeah, Yeah…

Let's face it, we either have what we say we'd like to have or we don't. Whether we'd like to have more money, better relationships, more confidence, or whatever it may be - if we don't the only reason is because of the stories we tell ourselves about it. We don't even know they are stories, as we are the stories, our lives blend. Just as the fish that swims in the water does not see, nor pay attention to the water in which it

Universal Laws:

1)Law of Luck
2)Law of Timing
3)Law of Averages

Use the laws to your advantage

swims, it just swims. We are in the forest; we do not see the trees. Humans are great story tellers. We start at about the age we can talk, that's why we're so good. It could start out with something as simple as our parents asking, "Why aren't these toys picked up?" The child searches for an answer. The stories begin here. After a few seconds we GET some weak just-starting-out story about how it's so and so's fault.

No worries, the stories tighten up with practice. Catch up with them down the road and their stories will be airtight -- even they will believe them. We are publishers and we sell REAL stories to REAL people who buy stories, period. We move away from people who do not buy stories. Notice the people in your own life and how many of them buy your stories. For most people about 99% of their peer groups are safe bets, they sell each other stories on why their lives are the way their lives are. It's a conspiracy we live in; you buy mine and I buy yours. You don't call me on mine and I won't call you on yours. Most are so busy concocting stories that they have no time to produce their outcomes. Their inner voices have already caved in and given up, so instead of finding resolve we find reasons or stories to justify or conceal why we didn't do what we said we would do, why it went south. What if we gave up our stories? The story of why we can't GET healthy, the story of why we can't lose the weight, the story of why we can't give up smoking, the story of why we can't make any money in this economy, the story of why we can't GET a job and the story of why our lives are the way our lives are. What if we just gave it up…let it go, surrendered to what *is* - without the alibis or rationale that it's the market or it's this or it's that? What if one takes total responsibility? I invite you to test it, see how it feels.

It feels naked, that's how it feels. It feels awkward and uneasy, it sucks basically. We just let go of our best kept secret to living in mediocrity - our *story*. Our stories are what keep us glued together emotionally so we keep our sanity; otherwise we would go insane. We've GOT to deflect somewhere. So yes, letting them go is difficult

Imagine...

That there were no such thing as failures, only results...

and uneasy. My story for the longest time was I'm "working on it," you know, whatever I was working on. I noticed I was always "working" on something but GETting nothing done. There needed to be "doneness" to what I had been working on, dinner had to GET served, yet I always thought working on it and doing it was the same thing.

How wrong I was! When I let go of the story of "I'm working on it" things came about, this book being one of them. I had been "working" on this book for two years and when I let go of the story I completed it in less than 45 days. The story does add time. We can GET away with delayed timelines if there's a good enough story. If the convict has a great story they can buy time, time out of prison. It seems most are out for the con in their living, setting up alibis, and living a conspiracy. One traditionally does not notice their story until they *notice* their story, notice yours today. GET off your story today and feel good about it in the process. No more it's the market, it's the spouse, and it's where I live. No more of I'm about ready to, I'm working on it, I'm almost there. Just drop it at once. We have work to GET done.

GOT IT

I GET it, letting go of the story is about taking FULL RESPONSIBILITY. Letting it go is a risk, it's nakedness…but it's worth it.

Quick Question

What is your story of choice, the default story you identify with best and what would it mean if you let that go, what would it mean to you and your family? How much of a better life would you have, how much more freedom would you experience? Are you ready to drop the story? Great…ready…one two three…drop the story….

Victims GOT run over; responsible ones recognize that they put themselves in front of the bus.

CHANGE WHO YOU'RE BEING...

For most, this will do it right here...

The quickest and the fastest way of GETting to your desired dreams and goals is to not change what you are doing, rather who you are being. The *being*-ness of humans. CHANGE WHO WE ARE BEING AND WE CHANGE OUR LIFE, plain and simple. We are always being. GET it? Human beings. Our doings GET thrown into the being, it's not the other way around. The being spins off a result. All of our actions and behaviors filter through our being and the overall effectiveness of those doings are then predicated on who we're being in that moment. If you took two people side by side and one of those people was happy and one was depressed and you gave them both the same doing, would their results be different? Of course. One is processing that action through depression and one is processing through happiness. Since we're always being, the primary question is who are we being in the process of doing, as who we are *being* determines the ultimate outcome. We are *being* angry, we are *being* grateful, we are *being* funny, we are *being* jealous, we are *being* passionate, we are *being* faithful, we are *being* negative, we are *being* positive, we are always *being*. To fully ignite our being-ness is to know that we're ALWAYS being. We're never not being. We're being happy or sad, being angry or depressed. We're being victim or responsible, we're being taker or giver, lover or hater, we're ALWAYS being. The day we quit being is the day we're dead, packed up in a casket and sent away to heaven. So the key to optimum performance is to identify who are you being while you're doing?

Whatever moment you are stepping into, "who are you being?" is the key leading question. You can have everything else all figured out, the full schematic to life; yet if you're not being the right person, you will

What new discipline could you
immediately adopt that would ignite
you personally and professionally?

not GET the right results. It's that simple, pretty black and white. If you are stepping into the gym, are you being the right type of person in order to GET the right results? If you are making a sales-call are you being the type of person that others will want to buy from? If you are searching for your ideal soul-mate, are you being the type of person that will attract that ideal mate? I used to think it was my doings, so for years the only thing I kept doing was change my doings, my actions, my behaviors, etc. and paid little to no attention to who I was being. The reward came not after I changed my actions but after I changed who I was being.

It ONLY takes Seconds...

It only takes seconds to shift our being from one emotion to another. We can go from fearful to courageous instantly. We can go from sad to happy in seconds. Let's say you received a phone call and you're informed that a very dear friend of yours just died; you would be sad. You would be sad until you shifted to something else, right? Let's then say while being sad, you receive a phone call from the state lottery commissioner informing you that you hold the winning ticket to a $20-million lottery. BAM! Instantly happy, poor dead friend, love 'em, may GOD rest their soul. The point is, shifts happen in a moment, the moment we decide.

Most look to shift their doings to be more effective and few look to shift their beings. Shifting your being will be primary. It's not as if doings do not matter, they do, it's just that shifting being-ness matters most. For example, if you took two people and gave them the same doing, yet one of them was being angry and depressed, and one of them was being positive and happy, would the outcomes or results be different? Most would say absolutely yes, and I would agree. You see, the being of the human is the central filtering system in which all of our doings run through. It's kind of like a water filtering system. If we took

What dreams have you forgotten?

clean water and filtered it through a dirty filter, no matter how much water (doing) we put through it, what comes out of the other end (being) is directly predicated on the cleanliness of the filter. If you want better, cleaner, more refreshing water, put in a cleaner filter, it's that simple. As a coach I am most concerned with who my players are being rather than what are they are doing, as their doings will radically shift the moment they shift who they are being. The person who is being committed will tend to do the right things. They're totally committed.

Years ago Andre Agassi hired my friend Tony Robbins to assist him with his tennis game. Now, Tony Robbins did not play much tennis. Yet he did take Andre from at that time about #30 in the world to #1 in the world. How? By showing him a better on-court game, showing him a new and improved serve? Probably not. You see, Andre already knew *how* to play great tennis, actually outstanding tennis, yet all of his tennis was being filtered through who he was currently being on the court, not who he was being years ago when he was at his best. When Tony and Andre reviewed past videos of Andre when he was ranking at the top of his game, compared to when he dropped to #30 in the world, who he was *being* on the court was radically different, which was massively affecting his game. At #1, Andre walked onto the court differently. He had a completely different physiology, he asked himself better questions, and he showed up as a winner. Rather than "I hope I don't lose," there were questions such as "Why did the other player even *show up*?" How must we show up on our own court (our court of our business, our court of our marriage, our court of our health, the overall court of life) in order to be most effective and win at our own game?

We all start as average and ordinary
and some grow into extraordinary!

GOT IT

It's who I'm being. Change this, I change my life.

Quick Question

Who are you being? Who must you be in order to GET what you say you are committed to?

PART TWO

GET UP AND GET COMMITTED

Most have wanted way too long and committed way too less, time to GET committed.

Success is simple, not easy.

WHAT ARE YOU COMMITTED TO?

Time to sign on the dotted line...

BE COMMITTED TO YOUR COMMITMENTS is one of the many things I GOT over the years of self evolution. The time of commitment is now; there is no more room for anything less than commitment. Years ago one could GET away with being lax and non-committal. Times are different, the world is different, and the world is asking that we all step up to a new place and GET committed at a new level, including you. I struggled with this one the most in my young years. I used to think that if I was five minutes late for a meeting I was committed. I thought it's only five minutes; it's not 20, just five. I'm cool. I was totally committed to being there at 9:00 a.m. but there was a train crossing through town and it cut me off. I was soon informed that I was committed, just to the wrong end of the deal. The deal was to be there at 9:00. I showed up at 9:05, I broke the deal, which meant that my commitment did show up on

What are you tolerating?

the right side, it just showed up in being late and not on time. I soon GOT that our commitments do show up, they show up however our life looks today. If we are fat, we are more committed to being fat than fit; if we are broke, we are more committed to being broke than rich; if we are sad, we are more committed to being sad than happy. It's a simple equation. Look to see where your commitments are. In today's world it's of utmost importance to GET committed to our commitments. Families' lives are on the line and jobs are in jeopardy.

Years ago I worked with famous motivational speaker Tony Robbins, which took me into speak at more than 3,000 companies, and move 25 times in five years. It was an adventure, although it was not always easy for me. In the early part of my career they wanted to fire me I was so horrible at the job. I started the job in the summer of '95, worked in-house telemarketing for a bit making $7.50 an hour and then after a few months they put me out in the field as a national sales rep. Two weeks out they pulled the plug. They brought me to the side and said they were letting me go. I was horrified; I had nowhere to go, no money and no resources. After some pleading on my end, they said if I wanted to travel to the next city I could, yet on my own dime. Well, I had very little dimes. I went anyway. I was committed, there was no way they were going to just let me go, it had only been two weeks. I scraped enough together to travel to the next city. I lived on my friend's boat, made prospecting calls at a phone booth in a local hotel and then took city bus transit to GET to my appointments, I was totally committed. I made it happen in that city and they finally brought me back on full time. I was excited, I now had a car, a house, and appointments set by the company,. LIFE WAS GOOD! After a couple more months I was beginning to get lazy in the field. Corporate requested a meeting. December 15[th,] 1996 I was being called into another meeting to FIRE me. They were calling it quits with me; they said they'd seen enough. My story was up. I hadn't taken responsibility for where I was, I kept blaming; it was time to let go.

Tick-Tock-Tick-Tock-Tick-Tock-Tick-Tock-Tick-Tock-Tick.
The End.

Well…There was no way they were GETting off that easy…I stood up, closed the door with a BAM and hovered over my sales manager's desk, looked her directly in the eyes and said, "There is no way you are firing me, I will break all records, do the unthinkable, and create a legacy, just give me one more shot." I begged. I pleaded. It was ok, it worked. She gave me that shot and I took it. I took it to the top just as promised; I broke all records just as promised. I took my income from making ten thousand dollars on a check to making over one hundred thousand on the very next check. It was explosive. I still guest speak with Tony's company and I'm proud to call him a friend.

What must you step up to in your life? What door must you slam? What promise must you make?

I GOT that *saying* we are committed to our ultimate outcome is one thing, and *being* committed is something totally different. Stepping into the commitment of the commitment is like stepping into the nucleus or the eye of the storm, it GETs hairy, yet it's worth it.

We must recognize and not fool ourselves into believing that if we are fat, we are also committed to being thin, because that's just not true. The truth sets us free. It's electrifying to know that commitment was the only thing missing and that I already possessed all things necessary to win, I just had to bring them to the table.

The facts are the facts…

If one is sitting around for weeks on end and does not have a job, they are more committed to being unemployed. If one is in a bad marriage, they are more committed to being in a bad marriage than a good marriage. If one is fat, they are more committed to being fat than fit. If one is still smoking, they are more committed to smoking than not smoking. If one is losing, they are more committed to losing than winning. If one is single, then they are more committed to being single than in a relationship. If one is angry, they are more committed to being

You are as strong as your
environment's weakest link!

angry than happy. If one is late, they are more committed to being late than on time. Where does your commitment show up?

Again this is tough stuff; this is not for the faint at heart. This is living with total responsibility and full commitment to doing whatever it takes to win and achieve in our lives. To basically have our lives work in the way in which we envision.

GOT IT

I GET it, my commitment is always showing.

Quick Question

What can you GET totally committed to having happen in your life? What have you not been committed to? What if you GOT committed to that? When could you start? Would that make a difference in your life? If so, GET committed!

WANTING IS NOT ENOUGH

I want this…this…this, oh and this.

I, like most growing up, wanted to achieve success and build prosperity; so I aimed to achieve the good life. I was told you can have anything you want. Just go for it, I was told. So I did. My wants GOT me jobless, broke, relationship-less and frustrated. *I thought I could have what I wanted.* I went along for the ride; I thought it was true…boy, did I go for a ride, and for many years, I guess I was slow. I was the guy that

Urgency is the Now; procrastination is the death of now.

kept saying I wanted to make more money, yet found myself broke. I kept saying I wanted a lasting loving relationship, yet found myself alone and unfulfilled, (ever happened to you?) I kept saying I wanted to GET my body in peak shape, yet found myself in worse shape and with less energy. I would say, "I thought you GOT what you wanted? I know what I want, can I have it please?"

I was beginning to feel set up and misguided. I kept reading all the success books and motivational books and they basically all said the same thing: just know what you want and you'll GET it, visualize what you want and it will appear. Just know what you want. I was beginning to feel like there was more that I was not being let onto. My coach would ask me what I wanted and I would tell him, yet GOT no closer to my wants. Just more discouraged. I was soon let into a thought-process, a secret recipe that only the most successful were in on. That thought is… *you do not GET what you want, you GET what you are committed to.* If it was true that people GET what they want then we would all have the most amazing life imaginable, wouldn't we? I mean who wouldn't want the "good life." Boats, trains and planes…If it were true that we GET what we want that would mean we all have all the money we want, the exact perfect marriage we want, the perfectly shaped body we want, the spiritual relationship we want, we would have it all. So since most people don't have all the things they say they want, that would imply we do not GET what we want.

Isn't it true people have a laundry list of wants? That list started at about age two and continues to grow throughout one's life. At Christmas time, the parents would say "what do you want?" we would say, "I want this and I want that…" Does that mean we are going to GET all of those things? Of course not. It simply means we want them, nothing less, nothing more. As we grow into our adolescence we say we want good grades and a lot of friends, and as we grow into our adult years we want a happy and fulfilled life. We seem to *want* everything, yet few *have* anything. I was one of those people. Just because the person says they

Life: Game

Birth: Start

-

Death: End

The dash is what matters most

Simple...

want to be rich does not imply they will invest. Just because the person wants to have a fit body does not imply they will go to the gym. Isn't it true that just because a person says they want to have a happy and fulfilled life, it does not imply they will - it again simply means they want it. Yet who doesn't want to be rich, fit and happy? Everybody does, yet few will be. What's the major distinction between the little boy who wants ice cream and the boy who's actually eating ice cream? One boy was committed to GETting ice cream. The difference between wanting and having is the difference in our commitment.

We find most do things out of their convenience and not out of their commitments, and doing things out of our commitments is the difference between wanting and having. I mean isn't it true that if one only goes to the gym when it's convenient they will tend to be unfit and overweight, and if one invests only when it's convenient they will inevitably be broke and living in despair in their retirement years? Most live a life of convenience and not of commitment and commitment is the key to GETting to the things we say are important. If we go to the gym and lift weights that are convenient with no physical struggle attached, then where is the gain, the push, the exhilaration - where is the growth? In order to grow we must demand, we must push, and we must go beyond. Most just want, and few go beyond the want. The ones who go beyond the want to the commit, live the life they say matters. The distinction to immediately begin to notice is each and every time you say you want something, be clear about whether you really just want it or are you 1,000% committed to it? If you just want it, the odds are you won't GET it. For example, "I want to lose 15 pounds" versus "I'm committed to losing 15 pounds" is the difference in how you show up to the losing of those 15 pounds. Most people's wants will disappear the moment it is no longer convenient and the person who is committed will do it whether it's convenient or not.

The challenge in our society is that people have been taught and trained they GET what they want; and the moment they don't GET what

Empowerment Question:

What can I do today that is powerful, positive and productive and moves me in the direction of my dominant outcome?

they want, they blame the circumstances, they blame the environment, they blame the conditions of the moment, anything other than their own commitment. Society has been teaching that wanting and committing is the same thing and so we blend the two as if they were the same instead of standing distinctly and separately on their own. We mistakenly believe that our wanting and committing is the same thing, never really noticing the distinct difference. Once one recognizes this distinction as the wake-up call of wake-up calls, then one can truly GET what they want by allowing this want to be overridden by their commitments.

GOT IT

My real power will come not from when I say I want something, rather when I say I'm committed to something. Oh, I GET it, my commitments supersede my wants.

Quick Question

What is something that you say you have been wanting for quite some time and you still don't have it? Could it be that you have merely wanted it and not been committed to it? Could you commit to it?

Empowerment Question:

What am I most happy about?
What am I most grateful for?
How am I rich?

DECIDE TODAY

...Once one DECIDES to succeed the HOW to succeed shows up,
it's like magic.

"How do I make more money, how do I lose the weight, how do I GET my marriage upright, how do I live my dreams, how do I GET excited, how do I feel more confident, how do I prosper during these tough times, how do I?" we ask. Simple, I say, just decide. The *how* to succeed does not show up unless we *decide* to succeed. The *how* to lose the weight does not show up in our lives until we *decide* to lose the weight. The *how* to GET rich does not show up unless we *decide* to GET rich, it's again a simple equation. We first decide, then "it" appears, the "it" being the "how to."

Most have it backwards. All over the world people have watched "The Secret" looking for the answers, believing they will attract their utmost desires if they use the power of visualizing coupled with the law of attraction. I totally GET that, yet the challenge is for most they have not *decided* to make that money or lose that weight or GET the new car, they have hoped, wished and dreamed, not decided. We have been trained to look for the how to first, then if we find it, we think about it, and then we look for even easier answers all without any decisions.

A decision is real. The judge has given his/her orders. If you're fat, decide to GET fit, if you're broke, decide to GET rich, if you're depressed, decide to GET happy. HERE TODAY ONCE AND FOR ALL, you decide. Your decision will take you there. Lots of people know how to lose weight, make money and have a happy marriage, yet few have decided. There is real power in deciding. To decide is to cut off, to break away. We must remember that decisions come first, answers come second.

Empowerment Question:

How can I work half the time and double my income?

Years ago while promoting for an event there was a lady who wanted to attend the program, yet struggled with finding a babysitter for her 2-year old. She said, "Let me find a sitter first and then I'll call you to register." I told her to decide today, register today and I guarantee you'll find a sitter. She registered and miraculously she found a sitter; amazing. I've had people say, "Well, I'd like to attend your event, yet I've GOT to see if I can GET the day off from work." I say register today, decide today and you'll find a way to GET off work, I promise. It's amazing how it works, it's like magic. Decide today and the universe opens up for your decision. Without a decision, the universe does not know how to handle what you say you want because you have not decided to have it, you've just wanted it and the universe does not hand out a bunch of wants, otherwise everyone would have what they want.

GOT IT

Oh, now I GET it. Decisions come first, answers come second. I've had it the other way around, now I've GOT it. Decide today!

Quick Question

What decision could you make today that could create real magic in your life, create real movement? Maybe for you that decision is to GET in your best shape EVER or that decision is to GET wealthy, or that decision is to GET a job or change jobs or increase your love life. You know the answer.

Secondly, who will you become accountable to, who will you publicly confess to in order to insure the realization of that decision? Remember to be at stake with your decisions.

When you drop your ego, you drop your front!

AS SOON AS…

It stops raining, as soon as the economy turns around, as soon as I finish reading this book…then I'll really GET after it!…as soon as!

"So when's the training start?" I asked. "When do you think?" the trainer replied. "Now?" That's right, it's in process now, congratulations. Life has started. When I conduct live events I remind the audience the event has started. At the opening I invite the participants to a wonderful evening and welcome them to the event and to feel free and jump in at any time. In the opening of the event I then welcome them and remind them the event has started, this is what it looks like and they may feel free to jump in at any time. Several hours later I welcome them to the event again, for those still sitting there wondering when the event is going to begin, I remind them it has already begun and to feel free to jump in at any time. It starts all over again the following morning inviting them to jump in and quit waiting.

Most of my life was this way. I found myself sitting in life waiting for something to happen before I jumped in. *As soon as this event takes off then I'll really jump in.* I was always about ready to soon begin to GET started, to jump in at some given point down the road, not exactly sure when, yet I think soon. Maybe this Monday, if not this Monday, definitely at the top of the month, then I'll really be ready. I lived the lie of the "as soon as" syndrome, the "it's almost time" plague. The severity of "as soon as…" had a major overrun in all areas of my life and did not exclude any one area; it ran through my life, it was interwoven into the tapestry of my life, in all areas. This syndrome leads to a stockpile of undone things, soon to be done things, almost ready things, as soon as things…as soon as the boss gives me a raise then I'll really GET after it, as soon as my wife is nicer then I'll really be nice, as soon as I make more money then I'll really start to contribute, as soon as I make more money then I'll start to save, as soon as I buy a house then I'll be really happy…as soon as I sell this house I'll be even happier, as soon as I GET married then I'll be complete, as soon as I GET divorced I'll be complete, as soon as I have kids, as soon as the kids move, as soon as I GET an

You must flex! You must push! You must expand! You must grow! You must go through the pain! Well, you must, if you are committed to succeeding, if not – relax!

education, as soon as, as soon as, as soon as…. Life is always about to happen, have you ever been there, I think we all have. While we're dealing with the as soon as, unfortunately we're missing the here and now present.

Do you have an as soon as? Maybe your as soon as is in regards to the market. As soon as the market turns then I can really start making money again, as soon as they're hiring then I'll really GET up off this couch and go GET a job. As soon as I GET my confidence back then I'll really start dating. My invitation is to lose the as soon as and see where that takes you. For most it takes them to their dreams right now because there is nothing to GET in the way, there is no down the road, there is no about to, there is no I'm almost after it as soon as…. It's immediate. It's now.

Neither the world nor our families have any more time for our as soon as, the world demands that we culturally and collectively step up now, not as soon as. It asks that we immediately lose the as soon as. Or you can keep your as soon as, hold onto it, embrace it and see how that works out for you and your family.

GOT IT

The time is now, there is no as soon as. There is no tomorrow. GOT it? Great!

Quick Question

What are you waiting for in your life, what is the as soon as…? How much is it costing you and your family by waiting, by putting off, by delaying?

Work harder on you than on your job

Do not confuse

It's not work harder on your job than
on you.

REFORMATTING OUR LIVES...

"Did you say I can start fresh?" "WOW! Just like when it was new..."

You've GOT to form your life the way you see it or it will form you, as it sees you. It takes courage, strength, fortitude and conviction to reshape and reform our lives. Your life will form you simply because it was here first. It will form you on its history and its well worn past; it's GOT generation after generation of supporting facts on you. You're going down if you let it, it won't let up, and it's GOT too much strength and momentum on you. Human lives come pre-packaged based on genetic code, beliefs and what the world has already summed up about life and the way things are and are not. When we're born we are simply thrown into that mix, that conversation. We are like a pair of jeans in the corner that GETs thrown into the mix to sort later. The world already had a thrust, had a motion, had a movement and then presto, we're born and we think we made this all up. No we didn't make it all up, it was already done long before we showed up. We just relive It, recycle it and regurgitate it, some good and some not so good. At times it's like eating cold leftovers.

For most people they're still in the spin cycle, spinning round and round repeating the same old same old. Doing nothing different, repeating day after day, lost in the grind, fixated on how it could be, but isn't. We find it comfortable, the well worn, the past, the approval and the rewards. For many the excitement is gone; half dead half alive, marriages are down to a mere exchange of data, with little emotion conveyed. It's down to mere existence and paycheck to paycheck. That's life for all too many. They're dead and they're just waiting to GET buried. No passion, no vision, no dreams, no life, no thrill of victory. Those days are gone they think. So what do we do, stay the same or step up and start to see it the way we would like it?

What's running you? What's got
you? What's controlling you? What are
you obeying?

Forming ourselves is about taking control of the past form and reformatting ourselves into an unprecedented future, one that wasn't going to arrive. We can opt for a new future right here right now by intervening into the vision of that future. We can reshape what we see. There is a vision we already see and we unconsciously live it day in and day out, this is called our life. Intervening into that already existing vision is one of the primary tools to reach and achieve our goals and dreams. We must reformat the already existing vision into our ideal vision.

We need to reshape ourselves into what we envision for our lives and the lives of those around us. We must see it differently, we know that. Seeing it differently will make it different, seeing it the same will keep it the same. If we look in the mirror, most see what most see. If we're fat we tend to see ourselves fat and if we're thin we see ourselves as thin.

Most keep looking into the mirror of life and keep seeing the same thing wondering why things never change. That's because the fat person must look in the mirror and see themselves as thin and the broke person must see themselves as rich, again basic fundamentals. You become what you see. It's in the laws of science; the movie "The Secret" told us that one. A few months back a friend of mine said that he had just watched "The Secret." I said "Great, are you doing it?" "What?" he asked. "I said are you DOING the Secret or are you just watching The Secret?" He GOT it. He understood the distinct difference. Whatever your dream is - see it, see you in action, see yourself in the driver's seat, take control. We must see that which we choose to have, it's simple dynamics. Although simple, it's easy to be tricked into believing what we see is what is. At one time we looked at the earth and thought the earth was flat; it seems we misinterpreted, it's round we found. It's easy to be tricked into looking into the mirror and seeing fat, it's easy to be tricked looking into the bank account and seeing broke, it's easy to be tricked by the con. It's easy to see the earth as flat, lost in the illusion, under the spell. Once we know the facts we could never see it as flat again, we know too much, we

Resistance:

The law of the mind simply states that what we resist persists.

are informed. We know it's round. As with ourselves, we must see beyond what we see. We must know we are powerful beyond measure, we must know that we have inside exactly, precisely, and definitively the ingredients necessary to achieve greatness now. We must know that and we must see that.

Take five minutes nightly before you sign off and five minutes when you arise to visualize your greatness, see yourself living your dreams and doing your dreams. See the winning touchdown, see the hole in one, see the family vacations and see the impact and contributions made. It's really simple, close your eyes, and with your mind's eye, you know which eye I'm talking about, the one that sees your fantasies, yeah that eye. Now paint the picture you'd like to have happen in your life. Do this every day for ten days and see how that works for you, it should produce a miracle. The miracle will probably be in the simple fact you did it for ten days in a row. Just do it, it's only ten days. See what starts to happen, watch for the miracle. A reformatting will occur; things will begin to be different. This is not voodoo, it's simple mind dynamics.

The sad thing is most can't be bothered, they would rather invest those ten minutes into surfing the Web, watching TV, or eating. Anything to distract themselves from being all they can be. Those are the same people wondering why their lives are where their lives are. Broken down and frustrated. Most will invest ten minutes into the Web, yet not

Bob: "I have no time."

Coach: "Bob, That's ALL you have!"

their dreams. I think it's supposed to be the other way around. See your dreams, live your dreams. See your past, live your past. Do it nightly and you will be living the dream. Don't do it nightly and you'll be living the nightmare. People want miracles and watching a sitcom will not produce miracles, seeing yourself in action will produce miracles. See yourself liberated from the shackles of your well worn past. You choose. It's only ten minutes for ten days. Break new ground; go for it, starting today.

GOT IT

WOW, ten minutes a day. That's 300 minutes a month, 1,200 hundred minutes a quarter or 4,800 minutes a year all of visualization and dream building - that's BIG.

Quick Question

Are you willing to invest ten minutes into your future if you knew that future would come about? Would you? Would you take the time to invest those minutes?

BACK TO THE DAILY BASICS...
Up and At 'Em Sunshine....Let's move it!

What are some basic, fundamental, daily rituals that you used to do that you no longer do? What basics have fallen through the cracks that

Thoughts are like E-Mail:

Send

Delete

Reply

you no longer even see or pay attention to? The essay, "All I really need to know I learned in Kindergarten" by Robert Fulghum is a great example of the basics. It's fundamental, it hits the core. Most fail here. We simply fail to do the basics, whether it's in our marriage or our finances, simply put: we cannot be bothered with something so basic and simple, so we search out the more complex. What a smart group we are. One of the major key elements of the most successful people in the world is they tend to keep to the basics, not that complex issues are not important, it's just we find that the most successful simply master the basic principles and build from there. In the military the starting point is called basic training, and that's for a reason, they start with the basics and build from there. The old cliché of going back to basics is good for all of us, as that's what seems to matter most.

For many people they tend to skip the basics as they simply believe that success could not really come down to doing the basics, so they look way out there for something easier. Really what is easier than doing the basics? For example, in a marriage, if the basic fundamental principles are overlooked then we are most likely doomed in that marriage. The basics of saying "I love you" and doing the little things like opening a car door or buying flowers are what the foundation is built on. In sales, for example, the basics simply come down to prospecting, presenting, closing and following through. It seems when most people attend a success seminar or buy a success book they are usually looking for the abstract ideas, the diamond in the rough, and fail to notice the little things. We find that champions, whether they are a movie star, a top athlete or a top sales person; simply are brilliant at the basics. They do the little things that make the biggest difference. When real estate mogul Gary Keller attended a success seminar in his early years he picked up a success principle so basic, so simple and yet so overlooked for most; and that was to think big and aim high, pretty basic stuff. Now, there were probably hundreds of people at the same event, yet Gary Keller emerged with the keys to the kingdom because he chose to grab the basics, the fundamentals to building success and creating fulfillment. This book is

I'm Strong Powerful and Confident,

I'm Responsible

And

I Can, I Will and I Must!

designed with the basics in mind and we know if you master the basics you will master your life.

What are some basic fundamentals that you can GET back to immediately? Maybe it's waking up earlier or making one more sales call or saying thank you after a meal or putting yourself in peak emotional state each and every day. Maybe it's GETting back into the gym or saying your prayers. Maybe it's visualizing your dreams every night for five minutes before you go to bed. Maybe it's setting goals, maybe it's spending time with loved ones. Again, what basic thing could you GET back to doing that would allow for a greater quality of life and add new dimensions to your relationships? Allow the basics to stack day after day, month after month as you are committed to reaching new levels of success.

GOT IT

Champions are not necessarily brilliant at the complex; champions are brilliant at the basics, the day to day fundamentals. Champions practice these day to day fundamentals and allow the stacking effect to compound one day on top of another day on top of another day.

I GOT it.

Quick Question

What are some basics you must GET back to? What are some things that have fallen through the cracks because of not paying attention to the fundamentals? What would it mean to you and your family if you GOT back to those basics?

Communication:

The quality of our life and all life experiences will be in direct proportion to the quality of our communication. Poor communication, poor life, rich communication rich life, simple!

YOU CAN SUCCEED...

That's a given, it's not as if you can't.

You can have your life work the way you say. You just can. Whether you're committed to going from failure to success, from broke to rich, from fear to courage, from scarcity to abundance, from indecision to decision, from victim to responsible, from taker to giver, from fat to fit, from breakdowns to breakthroughs, from losing to winning, from as soon as to now, from reasons to results…you can choose what you'd like to have happen in your life and you CAN have it happen, plain and simple.

The voices, the sounds, the yes you can, the no you can't, the past, the history, the multidimensional sounds of mixed messages and reverberating emotions of high anxieties, of whether you can or whether you can't do what you say. Well, here's the good news…YOU CAN…you can do all the things you say you can do, you can make it happen, you can live you dreams, you can do it, you can truly rise to the top, you can, I mean it's not as if you can't, you can! If a blind man can climb to the top of Mt. Everest, you can live your dreams. You can make money, you can create lasting fulfillment, you can lose those extra pounds, you can fall back in love, you can quit smoking, you can be at your best, you can get a job, you can live your dreams. Don't let anybody tell you can't do it no matter how far out there it is, no matter how unthinkable or unreasonable. You can do whatever it is that you say is most important.

You must believe you can already do it, you must. If you don't, then stand up and hit yourself in the chest (if you don't have breasts, that is!) Hey, it works for Tony Robbins. If you don't consciously say to yourself that YOU CAN DO IT, then your unconscious mind says you can't do it. The challenge about that level of communication is we don't even hear the unconscious, we just respond to it. So in essence we really don't think in terms of can I or can I not, it's really more of just a reaction in

Life: The Game

If we're not GETting beat up, banged up or bruised up, we're not playing the game, we're playing it safe.

our lack of going for it. We don't believe we can at the deepest level. WELL, YOU CAN!

Will You?

Again it's not whether you can or can't, of course you can. It's really whether or not you will. Will you do the things necessary to create the life you say matters? Will you take the immediate actions to follow-through, will you go to the gym, will you start saving, will you get excited, will you quit smoking, will you lose the weight, will you live your passion? Will you step up to what you say is important? Will you? Will you play full out, will you do whatever it takes, and will you tap into your greatest powers? Most just talk and few will do what's necessary in order to make their lives work at the higher level.

So we know you can, the question is, will you? Everyone can, few will. Few will do whatever it takes, most do whatever is convenient and then complain how they just couldn't. Most wouldn't do what the few will do, so it's not whether you could or couldn't, it's really whether you would. For all too many it's I can, yet I won't; yet for the highly successful, it's I can and I will. Will is a power; you've heard about it, it's called will power. Just like personal power, this is will power; GOD gave us a bit of each. The more we tap into them, the more we notice we have, the less we tap into them, the less we notice we have. Tap into your bounty of WILL and leave the legacy known by very few.

What is something in your life that you are not using your will power on? What would it mean to you and your family if you changed that and started using your own will power to change your life, to turn things around, to go from bottom down to right side up? Literally, *willing* yourself to success? It's your life, you either WILL or you WON"T and if you don't just know you always COULD. You choose.

Either you take charge and command your subconscious or it will continue to command you.

GOT IT

I can do it; it's not as if I can't. Rather it's whether I will or whether I won't, yet if I don't it will not be based on whether I could or couldn't, it will be based on whether I would or wouldn't, GOT IT!

Quick Question

What are three things you have been saying you can't do? Do you now recognize you can? Do you also know now whether you do or don't, it won't be based on whether you could or couldn't? You do know it will be based on whether you would or wouldn't, right? Great!

PART THREE

TURN YOUR SHOULDS INTO MUSTS
This is a must.

RAISING YOUR STANDARDS…
Raises Your Life

We must GET that raising our standards will IMMEDIATELY RAISE OUR LIVES, WE MUST GET THAT. This book is really about raising standards, stepping up and rising to the occasion and whatever else we want to make it about. Athletes are a great example of standards and how they play out. You can always spot a person with high standards, they just show. Our standards show up as a way of living. A standard is the life we live and if one is committed to elevating their life, one must commit to elevate their standards, simple, yet not easy. If

The Ax:

Must be Sharp for Maximum
Effectiveness!

The Mind:

Must Be Sharp for Maximum
Effectiveness!

raising standards was easy then everybody would raise their standards to raise their life, yet few do and the ones who do, create transformation. Let's keep this simple as I do not want to overcomplicate something as simple as raising standards. Again, clarity is power, so let's GET clear; a standard is a way of living. We all have certain things we should do, right? The shoulds we never seem to GET to....I should go to the gym, I should start saving, I should invest more time with the family, I should contribute more, I should start on that project, I should relax more, I should pray more, I should go to church more, I should, I should, I should. The key to raising standards is to identify your should of choice and transform that should into a must. A MUST is no longer a should, it's a MUST.

Don't wait for crisis situations to come up before you turn your should into a must. Make it a must because you simply choose to. That choice, that decision has REAL POWER. It now becomes I must start saving, I must go to the gym, I must do the project, I must GET that promotion, I must prospect, I must invest more time with my family, I must quit smoking, I must GET a job, I must become financially independent, I must. I just must. Tony Robbins would always say we tend to GET what we must have, and tend to put off what we should do. You can actually notice the immediate physiological experience when you say "I must," you'll notice it's concrete, it's certain, it's matter of fact, it's done. There is no power in "I should," it's weak, it's uncertain, it's vague, it's undecided, it's put off.

Test it, take a current should and instead of saying "I should," say "I MUST." Do you notice an immediate difference, do you notice a shift of absolute? It's almost scary because you know the only real difference between having what you say you want and actually having it is to make it no longer a should, but a must. Look and identify your top three shoulds and ask yourself what would it mean to turn those shoulds into musts?

Be Your Own Best Friend, Be Your Own Best Coach, Be Your Own Best You!

Not your own worst nightmare...

Create the Leverage

What would it mean to your confidence? What would it mean to your relationships? What would it mean to your ability to make things happen? Create the stick (to push you from behind) and the carrot (to pull you forward). Ask yourself what will it cost you if you keep your current should a should, what will it cost you long term in your health if you don't quit smoking, what will it cost you in your family relationships if you don't invest that family time, what will it cost you if you don't GET up and go GET a job, what will it cost you down the road? The stick and the carrot are a great way to turn your shoulds into immediate musts.

Own your must. There have been times I've been in bed and it's 5:30 a.m. and I say to myself, "I should GET up, I should go to the gym." Yet the real thing is I would rather stay in bed, I mean it's 5:30, it's dark and it's Colorado cold. The moment it all turns is when I create massive emotional leverage. I look into my day and see how I'm going to feel because I did not go to the gym, how sluggish, slow and groggy I will feel. INSTANTLY my brain fires off …"IT'S A MUST - GET UP!!!" Then my brain fires off, "you must GET up NOW!" Presto, I'm out of bed because my brain knows what those days feel like; they're terrible, they're not who I am, they're a lower standard than what I'm about. So again, it's simple, I did not say easy, just simple to transform our lives, just transform our standards. Go from a should to a must. Notice when you spit out the word should and take notice of the vagueness, the weakness it projects and in that moment, shout out, "I MUST!!!"

You will notice if you do this in all the major areas of your life your life will make the immediate shift you say you are committed to having. Yes, an immediate shift. The great part about raising standards is there's an immediate shift and not some down the road, soon, about to, at some given unknown time shift, it's immediate. There's an immediate action in

Clarity is Power

The clearer we are the more power
we have.

place and that action creates movement and that movement has real results.

GOT IT

In life we GET what we must have. I can GET to anything in my life if it's a must, GOT IT!

Quick Question

What in your life has been a should? How long has it been a should? Are you committed to making it a must? Great, see 'ya there.

IT WILL FIND YOU...

The Universal Tracking System

There's no way out of this….We know a lot about the universe, don't we? I mean we've been studying it for thousands and thousands of years, so we know a lot about the universe. Yet no matter how much we know about it, it knows more about us; it knows our every move, it knows what we're up to, it knows our thoughts, it knows whether we're excited or sad, it knows whether we've been naughty or nice; it knows more about us than we know about it or will ever know about it, it has a firm eye on us. One might ask how? It just does. How does it know when to rain - it just does. How does it know when to snow - it just does. How does it know when to go into fall or summer – it just does. How does it know when to drop the leaf off the tree? How does it know, well, it just does. How does a black cow eat green grass, give white milk and make yellow butter - it just does.

Without any reasoning, the universe basically has a GPS tracking system on our lives; it tracks us down and responds to our lives in direct

Most people do not need more facts, figures, data, theories, concepts or information; they just require a strong burning desire to win and be eaten up with it daily.

harmony with what we're up to, not what we should be up to, just what we're up to. Not what we show the world, but what the universe sees, feels and knows. We can con our friend Jack up the street about how life is, yet we cannot con the universe as it knows better. It's GOT a firm eye on you. It will wash you up in the sea or lift you to the pinnacles of success and opportunity. But you can't fool it, trick it, con it, pretend it, or fake it, you've GOT to do it. There's no getting away from the risk-taking or high levels of execution that are necessary in order to elevate your life or expand the miracle. You've GOT to think the thoughts that winners think. You can't think loser thoughts and hope you can GET away with it and still expect to succeed, there's no way. You'll go under the bus. One must follow the principles.

GOT IT

There's no way out of not doing it, there's no way out of not thinking the right thoughts, there's no way out of following through at the highest level, there's just no way out from doing it right.

Quick Question

What are you not doing at the highest level? Who or what are you trying to fool? How can our thoughts match what we show the world?

Consequences:
The ultimate learning tool...

FLEX YOUR EMOTIONAL MUSCLES…
GET a grip on this…

It's a basic law of fitness that when a muscle is not worked, it atrophies, it deteriorates. The same goes for our emotional muscles, such as courage, excitement, passion, love, patience or gratitude. Many people wonder why they do not have the passion they wish they had or they see in others and then typically complain about how they just have no passion, no thrust. The real reason is they are not going to the emotional gym of life and wonder why they are fat and sloppy in their passion or undernourished in their gratitude. We must work out, we must push, we must demand. For example, if one finds themselves constantly depressed, this is not by accident, this is by working out with high demand almost daily in the depression area, without any real force at all, mostly by habit. On the opposite end of the spectrum, if one finds themselves feeling excited and euphoric daily this is also not by accident, this too is by design. When Arnold Schwarzenegger was competing for Mr. Olympia in the 70's he would go the gym and wear his sweats and tank top to work out. The reason Arnold wore sweat pants was because he did not like his legs, he thought they were skinny and awkward looking, so he covered them up. One day in the gym he looked in the mirror at his amazing upper body, his massive biceps, huge chest and flared out lats and then looked down at his skinny, covered up legs and knew there would be no way he could win Mr. Olympia with skinny legs, so in that moment he GOT a pair of scissors from the front desk and cut the legs off the sweat pants to fully expose himself, fully expose his weakness. By doing so, he developed some of the best legs in American bodybuilding.

You see, most are spending their whole life covering up their courage, covering up their passion, covering up their gratitude or excitement, because they do not feel they have much to give, much to

Breakdowns create room for breakthroughs; one cannot have a breakthrough without the breakdown! Welcome breakdowns, just not the same one twice.

offer and so they cover up the little tiny bit they have. The great part about flexing our courage for example is when we wish it were there, it's there. It's available, it's at our disposal. Conversely, the challenge for many is when they wish it was there, it's not, it's nowhere to be found. We must spend time in the emotional gym. The key to flexing your emotional muscle is to flex when you do not want to, when you do not feel like it, when it's not going to be easy. A cigarette smoker knows that if they can walk into a bar and still not smoke, then they've GOT smoking licked. You see, anybody can do it when it's easy, when it's convenient, yet few will do it when the real demand is there.

The key to maximum growth is the more demand the more the growth. Find moments when it's down-out tough to be courageous, or to be excited, or when something seems to be utterly impossible, and in those moments flex your courageous muscle and excitement muscle and then you will train yourself even under the harshest conditions. The major part that you will GET from this book will be that in order for you to have all you say you are committed to having in your life, there will be a push, it will be a flexing of emotions, there will be high demand.

GOT IT

It's going to take a lot. If I don't push out it's going to push in.

Quick Question

What emotional muscle are you most out of shape on? Is it your courage? Is it your confidence? Is it your love? Is it your faith? What could you start flexing today and have it all turn around?

Everyone can, yet few will. Few will be willing to do what's necessary in order to GET the job done. Most can't be bothered.

WANT MORE TIME?

Here…I'll show you how!

Brett: "Coach, I have no time."
Coach: "Brett, that's ALL you have."

I thought I had no time, until I was informed that's ALL I have, is time. I have nothing else, just time I soon found. Have you ever wished you had a boatload MORE of time? You know, there just never seems to be enough time, right? Time is always running out, just flying by. Time just disappears, where did it go we wonder? We just GET consumed, life takes over, things vanish, experiences collide. Our daily lives lead into one big blur, moving past so fast, we never seem to GET a real hold of it. Have you ever been there? Time is an illusion research has shown and we GET caught in the illusion. We fall for the trick. Time plays tricks with our mind. We find ourselves juggling hours, days, calendars, promotions, etc. around time. Since time is an illusion we can slow it down or speed it up, we are at the controls, we can choose. We can choose to speed it up by falling more asleep or slow it down by waking up. As we know human lives are mostly asleep and so when we sleep time flies. Presto, nine hours went by. When we are awake time stops. Cigarette smokers know this all too well. For a smoker days blend with days, nights blend with nights, and life just carries on, never having enough time to do anything…every 30 or so minutes the smoker is programmed to step outside for a smoke, relieve the tension, obey the automation and so they do. Time flies day after day after day. All until one day they decide to quit smoking, to wake up to their life. A smoker's 24 hours is 24 hours, with no time to spare…and a newly committed non-smoker's day is 975 hours with lots of time to spare, it's the longest day in human life, it's seven years crammed into one day. Time stands still.

Life is not about things, rather who
you become!

What could you wake up to? Maybe you're not a smoker, yet how could you stop time and GET more in your favor of time, more time to do more things? I usually just tell someone to go find a habit and break it. Simply by deciding to GET off our automated habits it brings us aware. We know if we become unaware we will automatically fall back into the habit, so we know awareness is key. Staying aware is critical so we don't fall back into our automated, asleep life. Most are not aware, simply put they are unaware. They are unaware of time, unaware of opportunities, unaware of life. Simply unaware. Becoming aware allows for us to notice, notice what we have not been noticing, not been paying attention to, time being one of them. Begin to notice how much more time you have when you stop a habit and take control. You are not being controlled by time, you are controlling time through the power of your awareness and discipline.

Automation keeps us sleeping in our lives and waking up gives us time and lots of it.

GOT IT

TIME IS ALL I HAVE and I cannot add to my 24 hours. I GET a day, I can only slow it down or speed it up.

Quick Question

What could you do to slow down time? Expand the experience. What part of you is lying dormant because you have been simply unaware?

Habits start off as chains too light to be felt until they are too heavy to be broken...GET an Ax!

PLAYING THE GAME…

If you're not GETting beat up, banged up and bruised up you're not playing the game, you're playing it safe…

Working with thousands of people the one thing I have discovered is there are a lot of pretenders - pretenders who are pretending to be playing the game, pretending to be at risk, pretending to be throwing it all out there - just pretending. Well, life is a game, right? With life as a game, there's a start (birth) date and an end (death) date and all the time in between is the GAME. As with most games there are certain components that come together to make up a game; such as players on the field, observers in the grandstands, cheerleaders on the sidelines, referees, reporters and the occasional gambler. Let's microscopically examine the game and truly see how we show up to our own game. When we discuss the game, most people say they are playing, yet are they really? I mean really, are they playing the game or observing the game? Are they sitting/standing in the grandstands of life or are they down on the field playing their heart out, giving it all they've got, GETting dirty? I have found most would rather observe, it's easier; observe others take a hit, observe others take a fall, observe others go out of bounds; they don't have to personally take a fall or GET their clothes dirty. They can observe then complain, complain how unfair it is, how unjust it is, how it's just not right. The real thing is that most pretend to be playing when they're really just observing the players playing. The key is to GET out of the grandstands and onto the field and be willing to take a hit, be willing to take a fall and go out of bounds a bit. Life is short, it's here, it's now. No risk no rewards.

Besides the grandstand crowd, there is also the reporter group. The reporters report, period. They don't play, they just report the plays. They really truly have nothing at stake, again they are there to just report. Many people say they are playing the game of life, yet what they are really doing is reporting on the game of life, reporting what's happening,

Imagine...

Going from fear to courage, or from slavery to freedom, or from broke to rich, or from fat to fit, well you can...

reporting the good, the bad and the ugly. The cheerleader is the standout in the crowd-type person; they are cheering on the game and not playing the game. They are traditionally the go go go...type person, yet they stopped going many years ago. Most of these people stand on the sidelines of life and hoot and holler to others that they can do it and they can make it happen, yet they do not, for the most part, believe it themselves.

Another major component of the game is the referee; the referee makes the call about what's right or wrong, fair and unfair, just and unjust. The referee looks good most of the time; clothes kept nice and neat and are always right. Their only job is to referee and nothing else, just ref. They do not really have anything at stake, they are pretty much left fully intact at the end of the game. When truly examined, the only participants who really have anything at stake are the *players*. The referee, the cheerleaders, the reporters, and the grandstand participants will pretty much leave the game of life fully intact, fully unscathed. The only people who fully have it all on the line, are fully at stake, and are playing at risk, are the participants fully *playing* the game. These people, for the most part, lay it all out there. They jump out of the boundaries, take a few falls, GET busted up, GET down and dirty while the rest report, ref., cheer, and observe.

GOT IT

So my observation of players is not playing - it's observing players; and GETting beat-up, banged up and bruised up is playing. Time to take to the field - GOT IT!

Quick Question

What part of your life are you not fully playing in? Is it your marriage? Is it your health? Is it your business? Is it your relationships?

"Of course" answers we do not see, as these are in our blind-spot, and what's in our blind-spot we do not notice; and what we do not notice we do not pay attention to. These are called the basics...see what you are not seeing, notice what you are not noticing.

PART FOUR

GET EXCITED AGAIN!

I just was excited; you mean I've GOT to do it again? Yep! This time stay there.

90% OF SUCCESS IS GETTING EXCITED AND STAYING EXCITED...

Here...I'll show you what I mean...

We must GET excited AGAIN, plain and simple. We must GET excited right now. People have been beaten down over these past several years, it's been brutal for many. It's tough to come out from an economic beating and GET excited. GETting excited for most is not easy, yet it's the cure for many. We know that anybody can GET excited when it's easy, when life is all good and the world gives us a full hand. The question is can we GET excited when all S%@T has hit the fan? When everything went south and there looks like no end in sight? Can we do it then? Anybody can GET excited otherwise. Any fool could do that, GET excited when it's easy. Can you do it in the toughest of times, the harshest of conditions, and in the eye of the storm? Many across the world are going through their toughest of times right now. GET excited, find the opportunity. How? Ask better questions, and *keep* asking them. Ask yourself, what's great about this? What am I most excited about? What is my driving force during these times?

We just must GET excited, most are not. They wonder why they struggle; they have no spark, no excitement, no flare, and no passion. They know what to do, yet have no excitement to do it. Ninety-plus percent of success is GETting excited and staying there long enough to GET the job done. Many GET excited yet few stay there, and they wonder why they GET nothing done. GETting there is only a bit of the

What must you let go of in order to
be free?

battle, staying there is the remaining. GETTING EXCITED every day for many is the missing ingredient; this will be all they must GET in order to reach their outcomes. How do we stay excited? We must remember what it's going to cost us by not staying excited and giving it our all. We must follow through, and remember our ultimate *why*. Migrate toward other successful and excited people – people who are fired up to GET it done. Think about it, if there's an exciting hotspot in town, no matter how you are feeling, once you are in the mix, hearing the music, and around others who want to have a good time, your attitude immediately shifts to adapt to your surroundings. Bottom line, hang out with excited people, it makes being excited easier. GETting excited and staying there will be the greatest thing for your life, if you're not excited already. Excitement is in the eyes, it's in the heart, and it's in the soul. When you're excited the world knows, it doesn't have to ask if you're excited or not. It shows. You wear it on your sleeve. There are lots and lots of ways to GET excited, stay excited, and GET to your ultimate outcome, find yours. Your family doesn't have time for you to find your mojo anymore. They could hold out for a while, yet your while is up. Time's run out. GET EXCITED!

GOT IT

Motivation is the drive. I thought GETting smarter and more educated was the key - GETting excited and staying excited is going to be what GETS me to my ultimate outcome. Now I GET it.

Quick Question

What parts of your life are you not excited in? Is it your health? Is it your marriage? Is it your business? Is it your career? Is it your spirituality? What would it mean to you and your family if you GOT excited in those areas? Would it have a little impact or a huge impact? Great, GET excited today. Find your Mojo now!

One is either living a life of
maintenance or a life of growth.

DRIVING FROM YOUR PASSION...

YOU know...YOUR passion!

Do what you love to do and there lies your passion. You rarely have to GET motivated to do your passion. Why would you - it's your passion. For all too many they are not living their passion, they are living their nightmare, that's why they lose their motivation so often. Passion is in the smile, it's in the eye contact, it's in the walk, it's a feeling, a vibe, an emotion. GET back that passion, you know what passion I'm talking about. The "feel good days" passion. It's like the day you met your girlfriend or boyfriend, that passion. That sense of aliveness.

I discovered my passion at about age 26. I did not know my passion in my much younger years, unless you call drinking and partying a passion, because if that's the case I was very passionate. Do not misunderstand, I was excited, just not passionate. I've stayed pretty excited most of my life, yet not always passionate. It wasn't until I was about 26 that I was enlightened through a 3-day training program. My passion was found, the timing was perfect. The student was ready, the teacher appeared. As I sat there mesmerized by the trainer for three days I saw the broad impact this man was having on people's lives, I was drawn in, the impact was overwhelming. It was in gigantic proportion for me at that time. I said *if I could learn to do what he is doing I could die and feel really great about my life.* For 16 years I've never let up. I found my passion. I moved three hours away to go to a job and earn $7.50 an hour just so I could live my passion. I have been living it ever since, through the thick and the thin. We've had great times and no so great times, yet we've lived the passion. Your odds of succeeding increase when you stick to your passion. Whatever happens, stick by its side and it will all work out for you.

It's great when we talk about passion because someone doesn't usually come along and say, "Can you repeat that? What is passion?" We know what passion is, the challenge is that most have not felt it in such a long time they have become immune to its feeling, basically feeling passionless.

Your winning moment happens the moment you decide.

GOT IT

I GET it, find my passion again, and I will feel Alive again.

Quick question

What is your passion? What would you do if money were of no concern? What GETs you to put in longer hours or wake up earlier?

TODAY LET'S FIND OUT WHY?

Success is simple…80% is Why and 20% is How, most spend 20%

on Why and 80% on How…oops!

If you know *why*, you'll figure out *how*. Most just don't know why. The why is the drive, it's the motivation. It's the stick and the carrot. Our success or lack of success is wrapped up in our why. The weaker the why the less chance we have at hitting our mark. A cigarette smoker came up to me and said she was going to quit smoking. I asked why? She said because the doctors said she had cancer. That was her why – it's what she needed to push her to her how. It was her stick prodding her on to her carrot, which for her was a longer life.

What is your why? What is your why that is going to turn your finances around, the why that is going to turn your marriage around, the why that will GET you to the gym and feeling healthy? What is the why that will GET you to put down the smokes and throw away the bottle? What is the why that's going to spark your engines, turn you on and shake you up? What is the why that's going to GET you off the couch

Key clutch moments matter most, when it's you with you, the clock is ticking, life is watching. You dig inside and you pull out the best there is to offer, you step up and make it happen…

and into the job market? What is the why that is going to GET you to risk and throw it all out there, what is the why? What is the why that's going to GET you once and for all to make it happen? What is that why? Maybe your why is your kids, maybe that's your why. Maybe it's for lifestyle change, maybe your why is economic driven or status driven. Maybe your why is because it's doc's orders or it's just time to do so. Maybe your why is the pain of regret and loss. Maybe your why is to make contribution in the world. The more you can stack the pain and loss, the more of a why you'll have. The bigger the why, the higher the odds in succeeding. Most have the skills to succeed, they just do not have the why to succeed.

GOT IT

If I have a strong enough why, I'll always figure out how. Stack up my whys.

Quick Question

Why must you succeed in the area you say you are committed to? Why?

YOU CAN HAVE IT ALL...

"You mean it's not just this or that?"

Who taught you that you can't have it all? Who in your life set the example for not having it all, separating this from that? Who taught you life was an "or" and not an "and?" What are the voice commands you are still following, obeying? What is the example you are still listening to?

When one is passionate about what they do, one is with God.

Whose advice are you still following? What path are you still treading? Are you done or do you still need time to tread and follow? Great, you're done? Super. Are you open to possibility? You are? Great. Maybe, just maybe in life you *can* have it all, maybe it doesn't have to be this or that, and maybe that's just what we were taught. Just maybe. Maybe it's not success or health, maybe it's success and health; maybe it's not your dreams or your marriage, maybe it's your dreams and your marriage; maybe it's not your success or your family, maybe it's your success and your family; maybe it's not your happiness or your job, maybe it's happiness and your job; maybe it's not your spouse or your dreams, maybe it's your spouse and your dreams. Maybe life is an "and" and not an "or." Just maybe. We thought it was an "or" and now we GET that it's an "and"…I *can* have this and this and this and this…WOW, I thought I could only have this or that. Now you mean I can have my success and my marriage, and my dreams and my health and my career and my happiness….WOW, life just got BETTER!

GOT IT

I CAN have it all. Life is not an "or", yet an "and" - WOW, I GET so much more.

Quick Question

What could you add to your *and* list? How could your life grow by making this a personal creed?

Success is:

80% Mind-set
20% Skill-set

Do not confuse.

TAKE CONTROL BACK...

"You mean I can have control?"

THE WRECKING CREW: Wrecking crews go in with wrecking balls and destroy dreams, goals, and visions...

There's just no way you can do it, it's impossible. Just give it up, there's no way. Sit down, relax, just stop and quit. Don't you know where you come from, there's just no way you can GET to those dreams. You have no time; the odds are stacked against you. You never went to college; you don't have the credentials, just stop where you are. Just watch other people do it, there's no way you can, you're not one of them. You're too tall, you're too ugly, you're too short, you're too thin, you're too fat, you're too shy, you're too old, you're too young, there's just no way.

CHEERLEADER: Cheerleaders use mega-phones and shout positives at you to move you in the direction of your goals and dreams....

You can do it! Go for it! You're the best! Take charge! You're unique and special; you're one a kind, go for it! You're beautiful, there's nothing you can't do! Give it your all, hold nothing back! I believe in you! Do it! You're a take charge person! You're a leader, a visionary and a special breed, take a shot! The time is perfect!

These characters sit on our shoulders day in and day out running our lives, either into the ground or to the heavenly stars above. Who's running your life, the wrecking crew or the cheerleader? Who sits on your shoulders and yells into your ears, into your psyche, into your soul? The wrecking crew is there to wreck goals, dreams, and visions and the cheerleaders are there to push you, support you and GET you to win.

Success is:

Why: 80%
How: 20%

Do not confuse.

You have control over who sits where and who says what, the control is at your fingertips. Voices are heard to those who hear, and voices disappear when one is deaf. You can hear them or have them disappear. It's like magic; you run the voices instead of the voices running you.

Quick exercises: With your mind's eye imagine the control panel in your mind, and find the volume control located to the right of the main panel that says CHEERLEADER – did you find it? Great. Now, you may notice the volume is almost all the way down, just take the control knob and crank it all the way up to MAX volume, don't be afraid, really crank it. Great. Now just test it…focus your best listening ear and listen to the cheerleader cheering you on…hear it? See what you've been missing? It should be loud. Now go over to the volume control that says WRECKING CREW, did you find it? Great. Now, you may notice that volume control is almost all the way up. Yes? Great. Now take that knob and turn it all the way down, even lower, lower than that, matter of fact just turn it all the way off, are you there yet? Great. Now test it. With your best listening ear, you should only hear cheerleaders cheering you on, yes? Great. We're all set. The volume has been readjusted.

You have it set now to max volume for cheerleader and volume off for the wrecking crew. If you keep hearing the wrecking crew then you are hearing things and you may want to seek IMMEDIATE medical assistance, because the volume has been completely disabled.

The only thing you should hear from this point forward is go for it, do it, make it happen, you are the best, achieve greatness today, you are a winner, you are an example, I am your biggest fan, you rock!!!!

When you stand for something, some will stand against it, it's ok.

GOT IT

I can adjust and readjust the volume to either go louder or softer; it's at my fingertips. I thought only the skilled IT people could do this, I didn't know I had that control, WOW!!

Quick Question

What would it mean to be able to have your cheerleaders sit full throttle for the next 30-60 days cheering you on to your dreams, carrying you past the finish line? Would that make a big difference or a little difference?

PART FIVE

DO WHATEVER IT TAKES

Most do whatever is convenient and then talk about how easy it is...

WHAT AM I NOT WILLING TO DO...

Gosh, I'm glad you asked...I won't do this... this...this...this, oh and this!

Have you ever noticed your laundry list of what you will do and won't do? We don't normally take stock of this information, we just respond to it. We don't really sit around thinking about what we won't do, we just don't do it. Knowing this information is very valuable to you; it informs you of exactly what you MUST do to succeed. I'm sure you would agree that everything you've been doing up to this point has gotten you to where you now are; simple, right? In order for us to GET to

Success is:

90% Hard Work
10% Talent

Do not confuse.

the place we say we are committed to, then we must do what we are not doing, *not what we are doing.*

What are you not willing to do? What late hours are you not willing to go all out, what weekends will you just not work? What all-nighters are you not willing to pull? What gym are you not willing to GET to? What victim story will you not let go? What habit are you not willing to break? What pattern will you not interrupt? What diet will you not change? What sleep will you not let go of? What walk will you not walk? What right will you not be wrong? What ego will you not let go? What will you not let go of? What relationship will you not fix? What call will you not call? What book will you not read, what will you not do in the pursuit of your success? Come clean...

Write a list. To overcome the gap from where one is to where one would like to be is going to take doing something they have not been doing, a changing up of things. Look at what you haven't been willing to do and ask yourself if you're stuck with that or would you be willing to start doing those things immediately?

The times we're in demand culturally, collectively and individually that we do things we normally would not do. It's time to simply start to do things differently than we've done in the past, it's time to really step up. Start to do the things you have not been doing and notice immediate success.

GOT IT

The things I haven't been willing to do are the exact things preventing me from achieving optimum success. I've GOT an INSTANT TO DO LIST.

Raising your standards is about going from what you *should* do to what you *MUST* do.

Quick Question

What is it costing you, your family and those you care most about by not being willing to do certain things? Do you think it affects you and your world a little or a lot?

ACT AS IF...

Yeah, but I don't know how…

Spielberg calls you directly and asks you to come in and audition for a part, do you go? Of course you do. So you find yourself in Hollywood, sitting in one of the most famous director/producer's office in the world. You are nervous, yet you are ready. You have drilled and rehearsed many different types of characters and you know he will probably call for one of those. At least you hope he does.

Well, he doesn't. He calls for an unknown character that you have never practiced before, you don't know this drill. You say to Spielberg that you have not played that character and ask for a couple of days to prepare. "Of course you can have a few days," he says; "but we're hiring for this part today, matter of fact we have Tom Cruise in the back also here to audition. Also, the part pays $15 million. Are you sure you don't know that character?" he asks. What are you going to say, "let me think about it"… of course not - you are going to *find* that character. You're going to act as if you were that character. You're going to metamorphous into whatever type of person you must in order to GET the part, you know you can do it. If not, Tom Cruise will get the part and you will lose out on a cool $15 million.

What part must you play in order to GET to your cool $15 million? What are the character traits you must metamorphous into in order to

Be unreasonable and *find* a way to your success, as reasonable people already know there is no way...

GET to your dreams and goals? List out those traits and ask yourself, is it worth it to step into those roles you have felt unfit to play until now?

Yeah, but I'm not a great leader, I'm not a great dad, I'm not a great mom, I'm not a great public speaker, I'm just not very competitive, I'm not a born salesman, I'm not great at working with money, I'm not great on the computer, I'm not great at sports…

Well, act as if you are. Act as if you are a great parent, act as if you are a great leader. Act as if you are a born salesman, act as if you're worthy, act as if you are competitive, act as if you have that drive, act as if you are motivated - just act as if. You may not be able to do it right away, just act as if you could until you can. It's called fake it 'til you make it. You must do it, there's a lot at stake.

Stand the way a leader would stand, talk the way a leader would talk, listen the way a leader would listen, read what leaders read, eat what leaders eat, go where leaders go, say what leaders say, wake up when leaders wake up, watch what leaders watch. Be the leader today, not tomorrow, tomorrow is too late.

The world does not have any more time for you to GET better, your Spielberg is HIRING today. Pull out the BEST of what you've GOT right now, right here. Throw it on the table, Tom's in the back watching on the monitors. Give it your all.

BE A TWO-PERCENTER…

2% will do whatever it takes to succeed and 98% can't be bothered

Billionaire Art Williams uses the term "2-percenters" to describe achievers. He says two percent will stick to something long enough to

CHANGE is to modify, manipulate, alter or enhance the past, giving one a changed future.

TRANSFORMATION is inventing an unprecedented future, one that wasn't going to happen.

make it happen, and 98 percent will fall off the books; two percent will stay the course through the thick and the thin, and 98 percent will fall in the thick; two percent just do it, and 98 percent are talking about doing it at one undetermined time down the road; two percent do things out of demand, and 98 percent do things out of convenience; two percent are doers, and 98 percent are talkers. The 2-percenter is a very rare breed. Several of the top motivational speakers came together several years ago and created a 3-percent club. (I guess they decided to open up to the rest, and one percent more GOT in—probably luck.) Being a 2-percenter is a mind-set and not a skill set. It's about going beyond. When you go beyond in your health, you GET healthy; when you go beyond in your finances, you GET wealthy. If you go beyond in any area of your life, you flat-out succeed. Being a 2-percenter is a decision to play full-out and to be accountable to your results. It's about pure responsibility for your actions. It's taking charge and being a leader. It's staying open, because being open allows for pure intervention. Being a 2-percenter is about separating yourself with such degree that you instantly stand out from the herd. If you don't stand out, you are thrown into the herd … and when you are part of the herd, you don't get heard. 2-percenters work hard and GET that there is no shortcut to the top. They are willing to pay the price—whatever price. 2-percenters are urgent in their actions and have a sense of purpose in their prowl. 2-percenters GET that their story, no matter how good it may be, doesn't count; what does count is their results. 2-percenters GET disciplined in their actions and remain disciplined throughout. 2-percenters GET that personal development is the key, and 98 percent think more information is the key. I challenge you to take on a two percent mindset. What would your life look like if you were living in the 2% club? It's the few who do versus the many who talk.

GOT IT

I GOT that I can be part of the top two percent or by default fall into the bottom 98%, I GOT that the top 2% are a rare breed.

Things are not as they appear. The biggest illusion: Earth is spinning at thousands of miles an hour, yet appears standing still.

Quick Question

Who are ten people that you surround yourself with who are also 2-percenters?

#1 PRIMARY BELIEF...

*"Oh I see, just do whatever it takes,
WOW, it's that simple?"*

For so many they tend to do whatever is convenient, not whatever it takes, and then they wonder why they struggle. Success is really simple, just do whatever it takes. What does it take? It doesn't matter. Does it really matter what it's going to take to lose those extra ten pounds? Does it really matter what it's going to take to GET a job, does it really matter if you could become a millionaire within a year? Does it really matter what it's going to take to GET your marriage upright? Does it really matter what it's going to take to build your confidence? Does it really matter what it's going to take to explode your career, does it really matter? I mean all within legal and moral limits, of course. Aside from that, you're willing to do whatever it takes, right?

Of course you are. Your family is counting on you, the times need you and it's who you are. You are a do whatever it takes type person. The person willing to go the extra mile, the person willing to go out of their way, the person willing to do more versus less.

Go GET a Job With This Attitude...

This type of attitude will GET jobs all day long, employers can read this type of person in seconds, you stand out, and you make a statement. You wear this attitude on your sleeve, they can spot it a million miles

You either have a winner's self-image
or a loser's self-image. To test, just
check to see if you're winning or losing.

away. This do whatever it takes attitude raises your confidence, increases your certainty and moves you in the immediate direction of opportunity. You will separate from the herd so you GET heard, as you know your competitor will ONLY do whatever is convenient, they cannot be bothered. You are ahead of 98% of the workforce with attitude. You privately know this special attitude is your secret weapon; it's your arsenal of choice. You'll show up to places others won't, you'll do what others don't. You sleep well at night because you're not consumed with what you will do or will not do; you know you will do it all; you'll do whatever it takes. There is no demand or request unreasonable, you've heard them all and you've responded with lightning fast speed. You will beat out the smart and the super smart with this attitude alone. Your credentials hinge on this attitude and whatever academic credentials you bring are an after fact, a close second. You will meet at 3:00 a.m. at the bottom of the ocean floor for a meeting; you will do the unreasonable and unthinkable, you are boundary-less. Your rulebook has one page; it says "I'LL DO WHATEVER IT TAKES." No job is too little or too big, you can handle it all, your ego has left the building.

Think of a time in your life where you did whatever it took, you know that time? It's the time where you played at a different level; the time when you were hungry, hungry for success, hungry for wealth, hungry for opportunity, hungry for happiness, hungry for the good life, hungry to be the ultimate you. It's the time of our lives where we throw more out there with fewer restrictions. Do you remember that time? How did you feel? Were you more alive or less alive? Did you feel more confident or less confident? Are you willing to adopt this attitude to GET to where you say you are committed to GETting? Great.

I invite you to engage this attitude with full heart and soul, and do whatever it takes to win the job, win the health, win the relationships, and win the best you there is.

The answers are inward; do not
believe, even for a moment, that they
are outward.

GOT IT

A do whatever it takes attitude is the attitude of choice when searching out a new job, building or rebuilding a relationship, or optimizing my health. It's the attitude that separates me from all the others.

Quick Question

What would it mean to you and your family if this was your attitude of choice in all areas of life? Would this have a little impact or a huge impact?

#2 PRIMARY BELIEF...
There's Always a way...

Imagine each and every time you were up against a struggle or an obstacle and you thought there's just no way, it's impossible, I just can't do it - there was an overriding part of your brain and emotions that yelled out, THERE'S ALWAYS A WAY!! Find it, and we are encouraged. Someone once told me there's always a way for those committed and there's never a way for those not committed. There's just no way I can do that, you know I'm a single dad or a single mother, there's just no way. There's just no way I can GET a job, there's just no way, have you seen the unemployment rate? There's just no way I can GET that promotion, there's no time left, there's just no way. There's just no way I can live my passion, you know I have a job to do, there's just no way. There's just no way I can GET up that early and workout, there's just no way. There's no way I can work on my marriage, I have too many other things to do, there's just no way. I've GOT to go to work, come home,

Reasons, stories, diversions, justifications or alibis show up when results don't!

make dinner, there's just no way I can go to night school, there's just no way, do you know what time I go to bed? There's just no way. Never a way, always a story, the story of how there's just no way.

WELL FIND ONE...

THERE'S ALWAYS A WAY. Figure it out. The key to our commitment is whether we find a way, or find an excuse. Most find excuses and few find ways. Say this out loud: THERE'S ALWAYS A WAY. No. Louder. THERE'S ALWAYS A WAY! One more time....THERE'S ALWAYS A WAY!!!! Imagine when you set out to lose those extra ten pounds. Your brain shouted, THERE'S ALWAYS A WAY, even when you felt doubt and uncertainty, you pulled through because you knew there was always a way. The same knowing you have that the sun rises in the east, even though you didn't see it, you just know. You know there's always a way to GET the job, you know there's always a way to GET the meeting, you know there's always a way to make the money, you know there's always a way to create massive success, you know there's always a way. You know there's always a way to GET the date, you know there's always a way to turn your health around, you know there's always a way to find your passion, you know there's always a way to meet that person, you know there's always a way to write that book, you know there's always a way to have it all, you just know. You know you are seeker of the way, you live to seek. You know you are guided and led into the right direction; you live in faith all the way. You never give up because you live in the belief there's always a way. You live the same truth Thomas Edison lived in finding his way to the light bulb. You are relentless. You know better, you cannot be tricked into believing there is no way. You are a sharpshooter with your conviction, it holds up in the darkest of hours and the harshest of weather. It's unstoppable.

We are either painting a portrait of our future, or we're living old antiquated pictures of the past.

This attitude adjustment will magnify your results to what you are committed to, as before you just gave up, here you press on because you know you're 15 seconds from finding your solution. Your confidence will explode, your income will soar and your opportunities will be abundant. Congratulations!!

GOT IT

There's ALWAYS A WAY! I used to WONDER if there was a way, now I know there's always a way. This is my new mantra.

Quick Question

What part of your life have you been saying NO WAY to? What part of your life have you been saying there's just no way? No way to your health, no way to your marriage, no way to your career. Are you willing to believe there is a way? Great, find it.

GET IN YOUR BEST PHYSICAL SHAPE...

It's going to take a lot, you must be ready...

Most spend their health to make money and then when they GET older they spend their money to GET their health.

Really you've GOT to be in shape to take life head on, conquer your dreams and give it your all. Those out of shape have a tough time. It's tough to give more of ourselves when there's less of ourselves to give.

One must intervene, as powerful intervention is the key to Transformation.

It's tough to GET up early, swinging with all we've GOT, when we've GOT so little; so little energy, so little drive, so little muscle, so little determination, so little passion. This is the battle cry for most. The brain says let's go…the body says who are you kidding?

Are you in shape or out of shape? Be honest, in shape or out of shape? If out of shape I invite you to make a decision today to GET back in shape. As a matter of fact GET in your best shape EVER! Do the unthinkable. Can you do that? GETting back your shape will be like GETting your groove back, you'll feel 19 again and you'll know it. You'll want to wear shorts and tight fitting shirts, you'll feel great.

It's easy to forget many of one's issues will literally disappear when they GET back in physical shape. The issues and stresses of family, business and life in general will ease and subside. The things that used to push your buttons will no longer push your buttons. Our body will process things differently, and we will carry the information and stresses in different places. We do not feel so weighted down, so lethargic. We stand more upright, more erect. Our slouch disappears, we drink less coffee. Thoughts crystallize, wrinkles fade and we are more confident. We simply feel better. We are drinking more water, eating healthier foods, breathing deeper breaths, celebrating life more, our eyes are focused. Clothes fit differently, we feel great again, we've GOT that extra edge. We look in the mirror and feel proud. Our self-esteem has just been raised. We GET a bonus. We reclaim ourselves physically; spiritually we are no longer lost in the shuffle of unfit bodies. Our sex drive becomes unglued, it's crazy. We've GOT a hold of it and people know it, they are aware, it stands out. Life just got easier - easier at home, easier at the office, easier on the highways, easier with the kids, easier everywhere.

Those who are grateful are those who are rich!

The time is now…

Go clean out your fridge, throw out your old junk, grab the scale and GET ready. It's time to do it. You've waited long enough. You've GOT to GET in shape, you've GOT to GET back to life being easier again and you feeling better, your time has come. So what's it going to be ten pounds lost…20 pounds lost, what is it? Identify. Do something you can measure, not something you can just feel. Oh…I feel better….what's that mean? Better than what? Better than five pounds ago, better than ten pounds ago? Know how much you're going to lose and by when. The rest are all the details and there are many other books for that magic. Regardless of whatever program you decide to use, just GET in shape. That's the key. I'm not here to give you 1001 ways to get back in shape, just to push you to GET back in shape. Whatever program you choose will work, as long as your head is in the right place; it's all about mindset. I'm here to simply remind people to put themselves back into a physical place that empowers themselves to be absolutely at their best!

GOT IT

GETting in my best shape EVER will immediately transcend my life, creating true TRANSFORMATION. It will make life easier.

Quick Question

What would it mean to you if you GOT in your best shape EVER? Would it have a little impact on your life or a huge impact?

The key to a Powerful Relationship is simple, open, honest, authentic communication.

JUST SHOW UP...

"You mean just show up?"
Yeah!

Life is about showing up…it's not a dress rehearsal-type show up; it's the real-deal show up. Most are still waiting in their marriage, waiting in their relationships, waiting in their job, waiting in their health to really show up, to really bring all they've GOT; they still think they're in rehearsal waiting to go on…. One sits in the breakfast nook of life peering out the window of their existing marriage waiting for their great white horse. You know the horse that's going to save you, the horse that's going to rescue you, that's going to whisk you away. Never a need to really show up fully to this job as there's a new one on its way, no need to really show up to this marriage, there's a new one coming soon.

Always about ready to soon begin to show up, as soon as this one GETs fixed or GETs gone. Showing up is what we bring to the party when we come to the party. It's the separator between circumstances and self.

Think about it, if people showed up to their marriage like they show up to their golf game there would probably be some better marriages; or if someone showed up to their business the way they show up to the bar they would be rich and wealthy. If the salesperson showed up to the field as committed as they are when hunting or fishing they would be the #1 salesperson. If the dad showed up to parenting the way he shows up to his poker game there would be a better generation in store.

For years I didn't know there was this thing called showing up, I just knew I was always here. I did not know the way I was showing up is what GOT me here. If my marriage had issues, I soon realized it was not my marriage that was in question; it was really how I was showing up to my marriage that was in question. During hard pressed financial times, I

Life has Seasons:

What season are you in?
Winter, Spring, Summer or Fall?

GOT it was not my finances that were in question, rather how I showed up to those finances that was in question. I GOT that I was the cause.

Showing up to Opportunity

If life has an easier way, we'll find it; there are no two ways around it. If there's a faster way to lose those 10 lbs., or a quicker way to GET to our riches we're going to do it. We are always in search of a quicker, faster, simpler, easier, better way; and we'll do almost anything at almost any cost to GET to it. We like to take the work out of work, it's human nature. There are certain laws that will assist you in GETting there faster, but you've GOT to show up ….

Universal laws will take care of you…you can count on that like clock-work.

It's fun when you know the laws because then you can work them to your advantage, it's only when we don't know the laws that we GET caught with our pants down. We GET sideswiped, we just didn't know.

There are universal laws, gravity is one of them. There are other laws that are often overlooked. There are certain laws that work in your favor, they work to your advantage, and they support you. Just like the law of gravity supports you when you stand up, these laws support you when you show up and go to work. They are…

Law of luck

Law of averages

Law of timing…

Success is an inner game, and those who thought it was an outer game lost.

Sometimes you just GET lucky, period. It wasn't skill in buying those lottery tickets, it was pure luck. It's in your favor. But you've GOT to GET up off of the couch, find your keys, GET into your car, almost GET 3 speeding tickets, and avoid two car accidents all to show up, stand in line and GET lucky.

Sometimes it's the law of averages simply working in your favor. The averages say for every pitch you're going to hit a certain amount of balls, but you've GOT to show up to bat.

And sometimes it's just the right timing. We've all heard it millions of times over… "Your timing is perfect."

We invite sales professionals to go prospect on these philosophies alone, until we GET his/her skill sets up. The averages, the luck and the timing will pull in plenty of sales, until things improve. Although it doesn't matter if it's sales or picking up a hot date, or GETting the audition for the part, or GETting that job interview, these laws will be with you. They came with you when you were born, yet showing up is what puts them into motion, GETs the cycle started.

Showing up to Tony Robbins' Office

People ask me all the time how did you meet Tony Robbins? "I went to his office one day" I say. "You just went to his office?" "Yeah, I just went to his office, I just showed up!" "Well, did he invite you?" "No, I just went." "I did not need an invitation; I just thought I would go, I thought it would be faster than an invitation" - it worked.

Luck, timing, and my showing up played the biggest factors to that meeting. I was there, Tony was there, the timing was perfect and I GOT

Airlines Fly at: 30,000 ft.

Mt. Everest Peak: 29,850 ft.
Blind Man Erik Weihenmayer Climbs It.

What can you do?

lucky. I had no credentials, I had no resume, I had no referral, I only had my showing up and turned the rest over to the universe. It all worked out.

In Hollywood they say showing up is 95 percent of success. Just show up. Show up to the auditions, show up to the part, show up with all you've GOT, all you've become. Most miss out not because they don't have the skills; they miss out because they don't show up with those skills.

GOT IT

Life is not determined by life, rather how I show up to that life, what I bring to the party, my contribution.

Quick Question

How could you show up differently to the world so that the world GETs that what you say is who you are? How could you show up to your marriage differently so your partner sees a side of you not normally seen? How could you show up to your business in such way that your business literally transforms, no matter how good it is? How could you show up to your health so that the ideal health that has been about ready to begin BEGINS?

What is your code of conduct?

PART SIX

Building Strong Daily Habits

Habits are too light to be felt until too heavy to be broken…GET AN AX!!

INCANT YOURSELF TO SUCCESS…

Do it over and over until YOU BELIEVE it!!!

You've GOT to believe it. Years ago when Jim Carrey was starting out as a struggling comedian he would go atop Muholland Drive in Los Angeles, California, and incant his success, yell it out. He was broke, unemployed and hungry. Jim would incant he was the best actor, the highest paid comedian, etc. He said it was a way for him to deal with being broke and out of work. He would stay up there until he literally believed it. Then on the way down the hill he just felt like he was IT, he was the BOMB. Jim's first check was for a cool $10 million after doing this.

Military officers do these daily. Have you ever seen them marching and chanting? They do it together, they march it in their bodies, and they shout it to the world. We call them incantations, they are different than affirmations. Affirmations are when you look in the mirror and say you are the best, you are the best, you are the best. Although that does work, incantations work faster. Incantations work your physiological and neurological process; it's a real jump start to your being. The key is to say a set of rhythmical magical words than when spoken create miracles. Almost like magic. The key is to slam it into your body, you've GOT to

Do not hope for your success, you must insure it.

What are your premiums?

really move. This is where you will be glad you're in shape. You can't just stare into space and say you're great; you've GOT to put it in your body, not just your mind. When you say this magical set of words, know they are working instantly. Yell them loud, shout them out, dance to music, run in place, pound your chest. GET them into your being. You must believe. Here are a few incantations for you to start with…

"I'm strong, powerful and confident, I'm responsible and I can I will and I must!"

"GOD'S wealth is overflowing in avalanches of abundance, all of my needs, desires and goals are met instantaneously as for I am one with GOD and GOD is everything."

"I am a lean mean running machine."

INVENT YOUR LIFE THROUGH QUESTIONS…

"You mean if I ask myself better questions I'll have a better life?"
Yes…

Gosh, why can't I EVER seem to lose weight? Why does this ALWAYS happen to me? Why can't I seem to make any money? Why are there just no opportunities anywhere? Why do people always say no to me? Why can't I seem to find a job? Why are things always so hard to do? Why can't I count on anyone? Why can't I ever seem to get this computer to work right? Why do we never have enough money left at the end of the month? Why can't I ever seem to GET myself up earlier? Why do I always feel so depressed? Why do people always quit? Why can't I ever GET motivated? Why do I just keep on procrastinating? Why do I keep sabotaging my success? Why has my life turned out this way? Why am I afraid every time I go for it? Why can't I ever make things work

One's life is one's values in action, you want to know your values, look at your life.

out? Any of these questions sound familiar? Probably because we have all asked them at some point in our lives.

Questions shackle us or free us. We become shackled to the limitation within the question itself.

Asking questions is like pressing keys on the keyboard to your personal computer. Whatever you put in is whatever you're going to GET out, no exceptions. Our brain is unbiased. Our ego is self-centered, yet our brain is unbiased. It merely responds to input, yours specifically. When we ask our brain "why" can't we lose these ten pounds, make that money or GET that job - our brain simply responds to the question at hand, it's a simple mechanism. Ask and GET. Based on the question asked our brain says, because you are lazy and you never quit eating. We respond, yeah you're right. We stay stuck and shackled. There is no resolution within the question, only more story.

Better Questions equal a Better Life

How can I lose those ten pounds and have fun in the process? How can I feel at my personal best? How can I do this and enjoy the process? How can I go out there and meet my soul mate? How can I go out and find a job immediately? How can I wake up early and feel great? How can I risk today? How can I get motivated today? How can I make more money? How can I find and seize immediate opportunity? How can I find a way to have it all? How can I immediately raise my standards?

How to will provide a solution and *why* will provide a story.

Questions direct focus and what we focus on we experience. In asking the wrong questions we GET more of the same and with a new empowering question we GET a new opportunity.

You either will or you won't. If you
don't it won't be because you couldn't,
it will be because you wouldn't.

Notice your habitual questions to yourself. I said habitual questions meaning they are of habit. Habits you don't necessarily see, they just are. If you don't know what questions you are asking yourself eavesdrop in and find out, go undercover. You know the way you eavesdrop into other people's conversations, drop into your own. Find out what you're asking when you're asking. You will notice a lot when you start to pay attention to your own questions. You will notice most of them are disempowering and do not serve you. In the moment you notice the question replace it with a new and empowering question and see how that works for you. The key is to replace in the moment as to break the limiting pattern and start to create a new one.

Notice not just the question you ask yourself but the questions you are asking of others. You may notice many of those same questions you use with you, you are also using in your requests with customers, family members and people in general. You might want to look and see what your questions say about you. Are the questions coming from a place of lack and scarcity or abundance and wealth? Live an abundant life by asking abundant questions.

GOT IT

Better questions equal a better life, simple. If I'm committed to GETting to a better outcome with myself or with someone else, I just must ask better questions.

Quick Question

What would your life look like if you asked these questions:

What am I grateful for? Who loves me and who do I love?
What can I do right now that is powerful, positive and productive and moves me in the direction of my ultimate outcome? What am I really excited about? How can I do it better?

Look at life as an "and," and you can have it all. Look at life as an "or," then you must choose. Business *or* health - instead it can be business *and* health *and* relationships *and*, *and*...

BREAK YOUR LIMITING PATTERNS...

Quit doing the same thing, that's insane...

The Fourth Tunnel

If you put a rat in front of a bunch of tunnels and put cheese in one of them, the rat will go up and down the tunnels looking for the cheese. If every time you do the experiment you put the cheese down the fourth tunnel, eventually you'll GET a successful rat. This rat knows the right tunnel and goes directly to it every time. If you now move the cheese out of the fourth tunnel and put it at the end of another tunnel, the rat still goes down the fourth tunnel. And, of course, GETs no cheese. He then comes out of the tunnel, looks the tunnels over, and goes right back down the cheese-less fourth tunnel. Unrewarded, the rat comes in \ out of the tunnel, looks the tunnels over again, goes back down the fourth tunnel again, and again finds no cheese. Now, the difference between a rat and a human being is that eventually the rat will stop going down the fourth tunnel and will look down the other tunnels, and a human being will go down the tunnel with no cheese forever. No cheese in their relationships, no cheese in their finances, no cheese in their health. You see, rats are only interested in cheese. Humans are more interested in being right. Human beings care more about going down the right tunnel. It is belief which allows human beings to go down the fourth tunnel ad nauseam. They go on doing what they do without any real satisfaction, without any nurturing, because they come to believe that what they are doing is right, whether they are GETting their cheese or not. And they will do this forever, even with no cheese in the tunnel, as long as they believe in it and can prove that they are in the right tunnel.

GETting to the cheese is of utmost importance. Are you committed to being right or are you committed to GETting to your cheese? What else is there, a starved right guy? A bunch of EMPTY tunnels? We must

Imagine...

100% Truth Telling
100% of the Time

GET to the cheese, we must. The times we're in today are different than the times we were in yesterday, we've GOT to mix it up. Mix up our behaviors, mix up our actions, and just mix it up. Instantly drop away from doing the same things we have been doing…where opportunities used to be over there, now they're over here…

Habits, patterns, beliefs, automations, stuck-ness, ego, and righteousness keep one fixated on the fourth tunnel. Our eyes GET locked in, just like night driving. We go under the spell. We drop down…and we see things that aren't even there. For many people they are knee deep in that spell, seeing things that aren't even there, they're so stuck in their belief that it is there, they will stay in the fourth tunnel forever. When it's cheese-less, GET OUT and GET to your cheese!

GOT IT

When there's no cheese, GET out. Sounds pretty simple to me.

Quick Question

What could you do immediately in your job, in your marriage, in your health, in your relationships and in your finances that would allow for you to GET to the cheese, GET to the real satisfaction?

YOU DON'T HAVE TO DO THIS…

"Wait a minute…I thought I HAD to do all of this??" Of course not, silly…come see what I mean…

Do I have to or do I not have to, that is the question. Do I have to do this stuff here; do I have to take the advice? You don't have to! Plain and

As soon as...As soon as...As soon as...As soon as...As soon as...As soon as...As soon as...As soon as, then I'll really start life...As soon as!

simple. Life is a GET TO and not a HAVE TO, all the way to its core, it's all 100% GET to, with zero have to. There are no have-tos in any of this thing of life. It's a choice we make, a perception we have and a decision we live with. People lose their loved ones every day, they cease to exist in the flesh, they have exited planet earth. Yet, they would love to come back and be here with us, to prepare another meal, do another load of laundry, build another fence, mow another lawn, wash another dish, read another paper, pay another bill, clean another garage, walk another dog, but they never will, EVER. They had their shot. Time's up. They would love to take ANY of your have-tos, just for the opportunity to be alive again.

It's about Empowerment...

When we're kids we are told you have to go to bed, you have to clean your room, you have to put away your toys, you have to eat your vegetables, you have to do your chores, you have to be nice and respectful, you have to GET good grades, you have to clean the garage, you have to mow the lawn, you have to, you have to, you have to....ugh......

Do we do it? Of course we do. Why? Because we believe we'll be grounded if we don't. Good or bad, that's the way it works in many homes. You did what you had to do, period. We do it with a grudge, we do it with a silent growl, we do it with resistance, but we do it. Welcome to life today for most. Still having to do things...What if you could change that?

When we were kids there were GET-tos also. We were told you GET dessert when you're done with your meal, you GET to stay up late tonight, you GET to go on vacation, you GET an allowance, you GET your own room, you GET to stay out with your friends, you GET a day off of school, you GET to go swimming, you GET a play date...GET-tos

We will either have disciplines or regrets! Most have regrets.

are great, they're empowering and add richness to our lives. We *love* to do them. What would it mean if you twisted your have-tos into GET-tos. I GET to take the kids to school, I GET to do the dishes, I GET to do laundry, I GET to go to work. What if you just chose to do it instead of having to do it? Whatever "it" is. First thing, it would freak out your family and those around you and secondly you would be empowered through your choosing. Test it, see how that works. Just say something you would normally label as a have to and re-twist it into a GET to or a choose to. How does that feel? Do you feel more empowered or less empowered? Do you feel more like doing it or less like doing it?

GOT IT

Life is a GET to all the way to the core. There are no have-tos.

Quick Question

Who do you GET to become today? Who do you GET to be in order to reach your ultimate outcomes, who is that person?

WHAT'S NEXT...

So where do you go from here?

We're closing, yet you're opening, opening up to what's next for you. So where do you go from here? This is just the beginning; the beginning of being all that you can be, giving it everything you have every day, used up.

It's <u>all</u> a "GET to"

Life is but a flicker, we're here and then we're gone. Yet before we're gone we still have more work to do. We're not gone, so there must be work still to do. We are here with breath and life thanks to GOD and one day breath and life will disappear, yet until that day it's time to grab a shovel and dig in. Maybe your shovel isn't in the mainstream of business and maybe it is, regardless, everyone's GOT to grab one and pitch in.

As I write these words the world is in a mess of an economic situation lying deep in a world recession. Jobs all over the world have been cut and people have been let go. Families have been devastated, bankruptcies have soared. Companies have folded up shop and called it quits, many have given up. Marriages are collapsing at light speed and depression seems to be the emotion of choice for all too many. Uncertainty and mass paranoia are running rampant with little signs of recovery. Foreclosures are at record highs and big business banks have toppled. This devastation is happening all over the world. It's the times we're in; they are different than the times several years ago. Several years ago one did not need to pick up the shovel; they could sit back and drink lemonade.

It was lemonade time and now it's work time.

It will be lemonade time again, don't worry. Until then grab a shovel. You and I are a rare breed and we know it...we go the extra five miles, we do whatever it takes. We are committed, passionate and outrageous. We give back the best way we know how, by being the example. We know the world doesn't need more theories; the world needs more examples, the example of hard work, perseverance, dedication, contribution, passion, responsibility, integrity, and commitment. The world needs leaders, heroes and "I'll go first" type people. Society, our children, family, and co-workers must be able to look at us and believe they can do it too. We don't GET to enjoy the full gifts in life by not being the example, because then people look and say

There's always a way when committed, and never a way when not committed.

Life is a test of commitment.

gosh if you can't do it, then maybe I can't do it either. We just took away what they may have become through our example. Yet we couldn't even do it. Let us do it first, let us lead into the storm, let us tread the path, let us light the course.

The Time is NOW...

Set the stage, chart the course, unveil the plans, do what you were meant to do while here on earth. Never let up, contribute at all costs and stay happy and when the world tells you there's no way, say I already found it. God Bless You....may our paths cross through life.

GOT IT

It's not about circumstances; it's about what I bring to the game. It's what I pull from the inside that determines my outside; it's the man in the mirror. I am responsible for my life and all in it.

Quick Question

How can you immediately go impact ten people? How could you make sure others GET it? How can you immediately be in the cause of your life instead of in the effect?

To Your Ultimate Success,

Brett Figueroa

BONUS MATERIAL:

The Motivated Mind of a 7 Year Old, Grant Figueroa. For those with children pass this book along to one of your younger children for a quick message from my son Grant. Grant shares a message of empowerment to the future generation. Please note, this is unedited, straight from a seven-year-old's heart and soul, spelling, punctuation, and all!

If you GET inspired you can do anything. If you don't think about it and you just do it you wont be one of those people who don't want to give it a little extra push in what they want to do but they don't give it enough effort and thought. Maybe if you give it a little more then every body else you will be the best and you can be better than you ever imagined in your wildest dreams. Even if it is hard you can do anything if you just do it! If they think they can be better than you then do what I herd from a very good basketball coach just take it up to the next level and make your self better then they thought they could ever be. If you think about it like some people you wont be able to what you want because your not even testing out what you wanted to do your just thinking about it. Thinking and doing are not the same thing doing is doing and your using your physical emotions and thinking is thinking and you are using your mind not your body so instead of just thinking about it put it in to action and just do it! If you think about it for to long you will not even notice your doing it you'll just do it so do it now do it today so that wont happen to you if you do what most people do and just think about it for a little bit they will make it to a point to where they don't care if they do it and they wont become a successful person in there life even if they think its working out for them in a little bit they will crash and say man I wish I didn't think about it and I just did now I have no job no career no nothing but its not to late at any time you can turn a bad thing into a good thing like that just do it then and you can turn everything around make it a good thing and don't make it a bad thing if you think bad it will stay bad but if you think positive it will change everything but thought is not everything how hard you try is fifty percent of all of that so do both of those at every thing and try your best you will be the best but theirs always room for improvement so do more then you do after your doing really good so just do that and your good to go you'll have a fantastic life you'll have a wonderful family a top score career and a awesome job that you love every body will look up to you if you are the best and if you are young I'll bet you you'll GET into a ivy league college and you wont even have to pay you'll probably GET a scholarship to go there. If that happens to you it is a great life you should like that but if you don't witch is ok you just have to be your best and stand up to them and say I don't like this sometimes this wont work out for you but if it doesn't witch will sometimes happen just go away and don't come back. Whatever doesn't work out just let it go and move on just don't carry it with you just clean the bad things out and bring in the good things if you can't clean it out and its to hard like your favorite things just think about something else like your other favorite things and you only have to think about it for a little bit and then you will completely loose it out of your mind it will just disappear for ever. Now all you have to do is find a place you like and just make yourself at home do what you think is best for you and your family. Now you have a great life that is best for you and only you nobody else yours completely now make a good thing out of your life GET a good job A good family and a good   life   that's   probably   bad   for some people you will just say to them this is my home so if you think it is bad you can say that but you think differently we don't think the same that's your opinion my opinion is this a great place and I love it. Now go out into the world and explore find new places find a good place in the world and just have fun I'll tell you right now life is a place to have fun all it is is a big boat load of fun if it is not fun right now change it no matter how hard it is make your life fun that's really all it is to your life. You may have a hard job but even if it is hard you have to practice so you GET good at it and make it fun make your hole life fun and Just do it! Every body says oh no but I'm not able to make it fun its just to hard well make it easy oh but I did that and it didn't work well do it again and this time make it work do what ever it takes just do it! Oh well this time I did that but I still couldn't do it I struggled with thinking of a way to make it easy but I just couldn't well don't think about it any more put some emotion in to it and just do it now if you aren't able to think of some things to do to make it better then don't think about it and just do it if that is to hard because you don't know what to do well you can think about it for a little bit but if you do it to much you'll just stop doing it and only thinking it so plan it out quickly and then stop thinking and do some emotion do some expression in to it and do it now do it today and just have fun and you will always be happy for the rest of your life you'll be rich with your family but maybe not money but so what just be happy with what you've got you'll be very successful and you'll be happy I guaranty it. But also if somebody says you'll be happy if you do so and so don't listen to them because that's what they know but if you do like it you could do it but if they say this is what I like and if you do this you'll be happy do not listen just do what you think is best for you only you and nobody else you and only you if they say stop doing that its not good so what do they know well they know what they know and not what you know so just say you know what go away your not me I am so don't say this is not good because that's what you know so I'm going to keep doing this really all you have to do is stand up to him just make sure its fun its easy and you like it if they try to copy you that's their problem because theirs only one you not two or more one and that's you and you should know that but if somebody else thinks theirs two they have problems so just walk away from that person just move on and forget about it and never come back just move on and think about something else and not them so make bad things into not good things not great thing make them excellent things make every thing that's been bugging you into a thing that's making you joyful just make it fun. Really all life is is a big road sometimes you'll find bumpy parts of it but that doesn't mean you have put a million bumps in other peoples roads let yours be smooth from then on also don't be a big mean person and be a big bump maker let the other roads continue smooth not bumpy if they are bumpy they will do the same thing to you and you wouldn't like that so don't do it to other people. What you give is what you receive is what I herd from other people I mean if you are mean to other people they will be mean to and you don't like that but that's what it feels like when you do it to other people so just don't do it to them and they won't do it to you then you will not fell bad that you did but still you should of never done it but you wont do it any more so you wont feel as bad as you would of if you kept doing it so don't wreck all the other peoples lives just because one bad thing happened to you just keep driving and move on and be happy. I've seen a million people find a bump in the road and then wreck all the other roads they see through out all their eye sight and they wont become successful and they wont have any thing to do with their lives they will loose everything and you will be living on the streets like a flash so be nice no matter what happens . on the roads you'll find bad problems that hurt but they've probably had bumps to but because they care about other people and their not selfish like some people they don't wreck other peoples roads let me put it this way other people have probably had a problem that was just as bad as your problem so if you do it again they will have more bad problems then you so think about that before you do it but you could have a billion problems and still have a better life because it depends on how bad the problem hurts inside if you have more problems but they don't hurt as bad it doesn't matter you should help them and make them loose a few bumps if you feel good you will loose as many bumps as you want so be nice and continue like most people and be nice if you are mean so just do that and you will have a straight road like all the other people. If you have a bumpy road they will think wow they have a lot of problems they must have a bad life but if you have a good life you should say hey you know what you may be right about one thing but the rest is so not true it is your way of thinking so GET out of here just because I have a lot of bumps doesn't mean they make my life bad I always stay positive and hope or know that the rest of it will be paved and it will be smooth like most peoples because I may have a better life than you even though I have more problems then you or some people in this gigantic world the fact is your life is worse then mine just because your problems are way bigger then mine and you almost have as many problems as me and their a lot worse to so my point is just because you have more problems then somebody else don't go oh man they have a better life than me but that isn't true you don't know that until you go say do you have really bad problems on your road if they say no then you have a worse life but if they say yes then you hopefully have a better life but I don't think that any body out of the eight billion people in this world they probably have some of both witch is what most of you should have not only big problems or only little problems both problems so if you go he has a better life just hope that your road will continue paved and smooth and I wouldn't do this don't hope they have more bumps and not paved road   so just think every bodies will continue paved and you will have one too so also think about what would it feel like if this happened to me would it feel bad or good if bad then you shouldn't do it to other people but witch sometimes it feels good then you could do it to them so think about other people before your self. If you think about your self first you will have a good life and not other people and they are having bad lives and they probably don' t like to be around show offs if you think your so good but they will think you are selfish and you only care about your self and not the people around you. And they will not like you any more and they won't care about you any more unless like some people they care about every body no matter what happens they just skip the bad part in the story and make it to the part where it is a good part make it a happy life and have fun. Theirs never not any hope left you always have some hope even if it isn't good hope but usually theirs some good hope never give up but also theirs going to bad hope to but no matter how much good and bad hope there is never give up if you give up you will not know what will happen next its like a story book if you shut your book to soon you will not know what happens next like if you quit you will not know what is going to happen next in the real world so move on and find out finish the story. Make it happen and if you don't find a great thing every time you turn the page just keep reading find the happy ending just never close your book just keep reading once you find your happy ending don't stay even though it may be fun shut that book and open another book just keep opening good books and then find the happy ending shut the book after a little bit open a new one and star reading and explore the new book just do that and just find a really good ending and make it so it feels right. Make your self at home and close the book why your in there and make it your happy fairy tail and make sure it has a happy ending.

BRETT GETS INTERVIEWED
BY ELITE TV...

"Brett, the microphone's on..."

I recently had the pleasure of doing an interview with this fascinating and talented author and coach. **Brett Figueroa** spent time in the Tony Robbins organization, branched out and is now using his skills and talents to motivate people in business. Brett vowed that his books will be devoted to helping people both professionally and personally. We predict Brett is on his way to quickly becoming a national figure.

Q. How did you get involved with Tony Robbins and his organization?

I was at a place in my life where it was a must to turn things around in all areas, including relationships, financials (I was broke), spiritual, literally in all areas of my life...I was without a car at the time, I was about 26 and a friend of mine asked me to visit San Diego for the day and so being broke and just hanging out with my life, I thought it would be a great way to spend the day. While my buddy was at his business meeting, I drove around San Diego and the La Jolla area, beautiful place. I then remembered that Tony Robbins' office was in the nearby vicinity and so I made a phone call from a local pay phone and asked to come by and see his operations and they declined my request...I then thought, I must get in there to see what this man, Tony Robbins was all about and what did his operations look like...I knew he had transformed peoples' lives and I was in search of what he had. I then called back moments later and said that I was interested in attending some of his programs, that was a lie, I was broke, I just wanted in to the environment. I knew the power of environment, they then agreed for me to come over. While in the lobby area I was sitting there like a little kid waiting for some magic, and all of a sudden magic appeared out of nowhere and that big booming voice of Tony's was all very present. I jumped from my chair and went to the elevator where he was about to enter, I threw out my hand like there was no tomorrow and introduced myself, the person with him became shadowed. I was in awe...It was Tony Robbins! We walked from the elevator down the corridor to his car as he was headed off to do a Live seminar in Dallas Texas, I left knowing what I wanted...

Q. What did you do for him, and what did you learn?

I actually started in the telemarketing position setting appointments for $7.50 an hour and $4.00 commissions setting appointments for the outside sales team. I then went on initially to be one of his most challenged outside salespeople, who went on to almost getting fired twice, not once but twice. My outcomes were to move, motivate and inspire people and then sell them tickets to Tony's upcoming event in that city. I was a slower learner and really struggled to get what some of these other guys had, yet I've always been a workhorse, Tony would say that. Soon my skills picked up to my hardcore work ethics and I went on to break company all time sales records, it was fun and exciting. We went from making $10,000 on one paycheck to over a $100,000 on the next one. My wife and I moved 25 times in 5 years and ultimately I delivered over 3000 live company seminars. I learned to never give up and to stay with your passion! My passion has been to touch people's lives in a powerful and profound way; I just had to get good at it. I did. Most give up and few stay the course and the few who do, succeed way beyond.

leadership influence in other countries, such as Australia, India and Belgium.

Q. What are your future professional goals?

My future goals are to continue to write, speak and motivate people to be at their best.

Q. Why do you feel you have a "gift" to motivate and inspire people?

I believe that my gift comes out of my passion and early frustration to succeed and to now assist others in doing well. I've always had lots of energy and have basically stayed excited about the future. I would say God gave me a gift and I've worked on that gift otherwise He might have taken it away.

Q. Who has inspired you most in your life?

This is a very difficult answer as I have been inspired by so many people, people from all walks. The good the bad and the ugly, yet I would say the most influential person has been Tony Robbins. I was really showed a way of being and a lifestyle that was not theory, yet real life. I saw and experienced what was truly possible when one got clear about their outcomes and diligently worked towards them.

Q. what would you say to something who procrastinates and is not reaching their career potential?

First of all, clarity is power and the more clear someone is the more power someone has…most are just not clear and so they put off, delay and procrastinate. The key is to get clear on what you truly want in all areas of life, put a strategy together, align with the people who will assist you in getting there, take massive action in that direction, notice if your actions are getting you closer or further away to your outcome, manipulate where necessary and never ever give up.

Q. Do you feel helping people achieve success in their professional life also helps them in their personal lives?

Yes, it gives them confidence to succeed in other places where they have not been succeeding. Jim Rohn the motivational speaker says "work harder on yourself than on your job" - if one works hard on their job, they'll make a living and yet working harder on yourself can make you a fortune! Working harder on their confidence, their self esteem, their actions, their courage, their passion, working on the inner equities seem to pay off massive rewards compared to working on the superficial outer stuff.

Q. Do you feel we all need a life coach of some kind?

No, I do not believe we need one, I do believe those who are committed to succeeding usually choose to have one. The people who need a life coach usually come to the table as needy and coaching needy people is a tough business, yet for those who truly are committed to a greater way of life, then absolutely having a coach is a must.

Q. Where do you see yourself in 10 years?

In ten years from now, that would be 2019, I see myself as an extremely influential figure in the world helping others to become more, I've had thoughts of having my own T.V success talk show as to where I can interview successful business and life leaders, so this is a possibility. I see my family and I traveling around the world touching lives and making an impact and just having fun. I see myself being deeply in love with my family, life and continuing to live my passion.